A Little Dose of Mercy of Jesus

Volume 1

CeCe

Dedication

To everyone who reads the books that my niece shares with the readers. These include stories that describe her life through these dedicated books. I would like to say that it's an honor, a pleasure, and a privilege to share with you my thoughts about my niece, and also to offer her my congratulations on her books that she puts forth to give God the Praise and Glory on His healing within her life and the others that provide her the testimonies of their healing and blessings as well.

She has always been a very kind-hearted and thoughtful person. I believe she was born with an entrepreneurial spirit. From early adulthood, she pursued her calling unto God. She has spent mostly all of her life supplying uniforms, which put her in one of the best places that she could have been. Doing this job allowed her to meet people from all areas of the government. The task also allowed her to get to know some of the different spirits of God in working. They may have good jobs, but life task still hits everyone the same way. Her stories share the things that people shared with her, as the story about her uncle and me in this book. My niece is a born again Christian and truly spends her time sharing the word of God freely within her church and work, and everywhere she goes. She has spent time sharing and bring the same love of God to our church too, which is The Word of God Fellowship and Christian Center Church at 1610 Main Street, Conyers Georgia where her Uncle John T. Smith is the Pastor and I the First Lady Catherine Smith.

She always brings people to worship with us when she visits us. She has had many challenges within her life, this is so true, yet God has kept her through it all, and He will do the same thing for you as well if you trust and believe in the spirit of God and let him take control within your life as well. He is the one and only true living God, and he's always the same, yesterday, today, tomorrow, and forever more if you trust and believe in him. To God, be the Glory for He has done great works within her life and is still doing greater works, as she grows more within the spirit of God in her life.

Auntie, First Lady Catherine Smith
Word of God fellowship and Christian Center

Acknowledgment

This book goes to the parents that God had given me. They both have passed on to be with the Lord, in the flesh, but living in my spirit daily. I walk under the anointing of leadership from them for sure. God placed these parents within my life for seeking knowledge and as His Blessings. They taught me to serve Him within everything I do.

The continuing Blessing of the healing and God within other people lives as well. We walk in the unity of God to give back today's blessings by doing our duties. We promote Jesus' healing and blessing openly unto the world for faith, healing blessing, and relief of the daily tasks within our lives today. It's truly the same God!

He did it in the days of the Bible, and He's doing it today if we only believe and trust Him. God never leaves us alone, as he's always there for us in our daily tasks present in our lives; no matter how hard or bad they are, he's there for us. We are not alone, but others are dealing with the same problems that we face today. We are not talking to them, and they are not talking to us as well. That's where *A Little Dose of Jesus* is born from; helping one another throw the eyes of Christ daily—leading each other with the promises and faith for one another by believing in Christ. Helping our brothers and sisters stay strong within the words of Christ for us should be the True goal.

Helping tear down the walls of disbelief within someone else's life for the healing of Christ. He did it for me, and I'm not special! He'll do it for anyone else according to their will and trust in God. I'm a steadfast believer in the healing and power of God, for everyone's life with Him. I'm sharing stories of my walk of faith and blessings that I have enjoyed. The same must have crossed someone else' path in Christ as well; if we only give it to Him!

About The Author

CeCe is a servant of God. A true servant. Now in my speaking, but living in my everyday walk. For God, has had favor all over my life. He has showed me who he is within my life. The guidance of Christ for healing and blessing of him. To restore everything that the devil stole from me within my life. I don't look like all the things that took place within my life. My life has had so many ups and downs, But God. But the healing and Blessing of God. Yet still having the faith to overcome whatever was placed in my way.

The grace to keep the faith in God regardless of the pain that I was feeling. Theirs scare on my natural body as a reminder of how far that I have come and the healing from the test that I just passed in Christ for example when I attend Christ to fellowship among the saints of God, I'm always waving my left hand, yet I'm right handed. Just to let God know how much I thank him for them healing from being paralyze on my left. For yet today, I can use my left arm and leg. Being able to walk again, without a walker or cane.

Being able to wave unto him in praise for doing what doctors said that I'll never be able to do again, without them. For standing on the words of God in trust and belief that he'll do it for me. Holding him to his word for the asking. It didn't happen in a day nor a week. It took some time and truly I don't remember as to how long, but it happen, just like he said it would was my outcome. And that's more than enough for one's healing.

Today I move as I did twenty years ago. Still have some shortcomings to keep me praying for relief in him. Just give your cares to the Lord and leave them there. Don't go back and pick them up because you feel he's not moving fast enough. Just wait on God's relief for your favor in your life of him.

He won't run out on you so, don't run out on him, but stand still on the voice of God for your own healing and blessing of him. If he did it for me, and I'm no better than you? He's waiting on you. Come let's go have a Holy Ghost time in the Lord. Giving true praise where praise is due. Millions of people give praise to the wrong one's all the time. Why? Because they look like the one that they are looking at in the mirror and they are truly their

God for sure. They drop their names as if they are the healer the savior and the one covering them? I find something wrong with that, for sure. The living and true God, we can't even breathe without him and that's were they are lost. The titles that man give himself means nothing without Christ in his life for real. The material things that they have accomplish before people, stands for nothing when Christ isn't in it. The list goes on. No God, No peace and it just does make since to go to hell through the Church? But then we must also realize the reason Jesus had shut the church down? Today, the churches aren't much better either. They are big network marking places. They do more clicks groups as well. Their no unity among the people.

They spend more time on things that has nothing to do with the salvation of God's people than anything. The people are still lost for the lack of knowledge of the Christ, yet technology has the whole world within people hands? Food for thought, If the people of God, was carrying themselves in the same Godly matter that they treasure their phones, what a wonderful world this would be. Instead they carry themselves as world does, instead of being in the world and not of the world but Christ

Contents

Page Left Blank Intentionally

Chapter 1
Just Doing Some Thinking

I found myself telling someone about how selfish I've become. The truth is you can't buy happiness or love, and I know this so well that I can't sell myself on the lies of men anymore. From now on, I'm going to be good to me because I know outside of me there is Jesus, and that's more than enough for anyone. I don't know why men tease women when they know that they can't please anyone, not even themselves. The pain is written all over their faces while their pockets are only one dollar away from being broke.

If they cannot even take care of themselves, how are they going to take care of you when you become their responsibility? I just know that they can't but it sure sounds good to those women who buy truckloads from them and become attached. I'm just not foolish enough to go for it. This game never change just the faces do. The younger they are, the smarter they think that they are and the bigger fool they think you are.

Well this is what I do, I do a lot of watching even when I'm not praying, and that's because of my father. I have the wisdom to know the difference, and I can't say everybody had parents like mine, but I do thank God for the parents that He gave to me. My dad was a legend in his own special way. People who came across him always said that he would leave an everlasting impression on them.

Some for the good and difficult for others, but at any rate, they never forgot him, ever. I'm the same way as well. There are many people who might dislike me. I would say that the number of people who dislike me is three times more than people who love me for who I am. My behavior and thinking always show up transparently.

The love and kindness that many people give to me are priceless. Today, it stormed, and they shut down the bus and train system and most of the state; but that didn't stop me! I went to work as I do daily with Jesus on my side and had customers as well. They saw my car and came into the shop to chat or even help me work. Now, look at the love of God in them for me. Now as I am just like my father, I sometimes say things to really put some thought on a person's mind. We say things to make you think and think hard. It often happens that people come back to talk to me about something that I said to them last week, and it's still on their minds. And then I give them some more to think about the same topic. Sometimes, I may have said something funny, but usually, I deliver messages that are food for thought. I believe that often God puts in my spirit to correct whatever is going on wrong in their lives, because in truth I don't know, and I don't ask either.

Sometimes they go straight to the point, and other times they never say but tell me that they needed that today. I've seen times they wanted just to blow their brains out, but by the time I finish with them, they have changed their minds about taking their lives, their selves for that matter. That's the way God works. He puts people within your life for the time you need them the most, if for nothing else to give you hope for a greater tomorrow. That's the power of all mighty God for our growth and faith in life. And He doesn't care who he uses to reach you, just as long as you get the divine message and mercy.

God will use anyone to help get us back on the right track. Sometimes we don't know how to receive what God has planned for us. We find ourselves trapped in the foolishness that people lay out for us, and we don't know how to cut our sin ties and move forward within our life. Some of us lose our lives because we commit suicide as an easy way out, but God doesn't honor it at all. He may give you free will within your life to do as you may, but he doesn't respect it. I guess you know the rest of that.

Looking for the Hook Up

People sometimes look for the short cut in everything or should I say they are always looking for the cheapest way of doing all things in their life. I know some people that live to use coupons. Well, I think that in most cases if you wait for it to go on sale, the best things are already gone, and you're getting what's left over by people. If I can't afford to buy it at regular price, it must not be within my reach. They run with food coupons to the grocery store and restaurants to places they like to eat or ask you to split a meal with them; but if I couldn't afford to eat there, I wouldn't be in there in the first place? When we go shopping for clothes, they have coupons and hit all the clearance racks. There is nothing wrong with looking for a bargain sometimes, but all the time, now that's something else. And when it comes to God, they are the same way.

They get in the hundred dollar line but put two dollars in the envelope, without their name on it and wonder why they work so hard, but they're never truly blessed. You can't rob God, and you're surely a fool to try by impressing men. Oh, they should save their front stage act for the lights and cameras, but God knows all of the foolishness that man didn't see. He has it recorded in the book of life with your name on it.

My Arrival in Detroit

Now I'm visiting my Godchild in Detroit. The city houses so many big and beautiful churches. I'm sorry that I didn't get to worship on this trip. Usually, when I go out of town, I find myself a place to go worship because I love to watch people worship God in other languages and states as well.

Of course, this wasn't the case in Detroit, but my flight back was at eight-thirty in the morning, and I didn't really want to spend the money to change the schedule. But as I went sightseeing through Detroit, I had the pleasure of seeing so many beautiful churches on the outside, yet I was wondering what was being taught inside these places of worship. I firmly believe that's what's really important, what the people are being fed for food for the soul and who is feeding them and lending them as well.

Things are never as they might look on the outside, but you must get on the inside to see and feel the spirit of God moving in His people. You can't fool me with the singing and empty preaching, but I look at the fruit that the person is bearing before me. Sometimes I don't see any good fruit, and I know something is definitely wrong in that place. God has a way of letting you know who's who and what they are doing if you're in a relationship with him. I sat through my Godchild's graduation for her Bachelor's degree in business, and she is also going on to get her Master's degree in business as well. Well, I was looking at her as she has grown so much in the last few years.

She wants to make something out of herself, and she had plenty of other choices that she could have undertaken. Things haven't always been easy for her, but she made a complete U-turn within her life. I know she has so many more mountains to climb, but I firmly believe that she's going to make it; and I'll be at the next graduation as well.

When you see someone trying you should stand up behind them and push them as hard as you can for their own good. This is what I did this weekend, out of love. I know I made her mad, and I wanted her to be as well, angry enough to make some more shift changes within her life. Making her mad got her started on the road that she's on now.

Telling her to go back and rewrite her plans got them changed three sixty degrees and got her on the road that she's on now. I pushed her some more, as I know she can take it all! I know she's not going too quickly because it's not in her. She just needs some pushing in the right directions, and she'll do the rest. Detroit was a lot cleaner than I thought it would be. Coming from New York and back when I left New York, it was a big run down city, and I guess all the old places like Ohio, Chicago, Detroit, and New York are all ancient cities and people run them down. But I don't get out as much anymore, and they are totally different today when compared from their look a few decades ago. They all got new buildings, malls, and other neat stuff. The people in general, all look the same as well. Dyeing their hair crazy colors and doing the tattoos and the crazy body piercings as well. The fashion of it all lost me because I am not going to be able to do it, not to my body, not at all.

As I traveled, I realized how much I genuinely don't see. The way the world has changed on every end. People don't even look the same, not judging but definitely not for their good. It seems as if the body piercings and tattoos have taken the world over by storm. These shops seem to be as popular as the grocery stores on every corner and for what? Many people wish that they hadn't done it after a few years, and what it costs to remove something that God didn't want for you anyway. We do so much by calling it a fashion, but fashion quickly fades, and you're still caught up from one thing to another without honestly thinking about what you are doing. And the biggest question is why you are doing it to yourself. I see people put the so-called lovers on their body and think that they will be together a lifetime, and they are now gone after a while? When I see you put two or three names on your body, and they are now all gone; I question what could you have been thinking about and how you actually live with that daily. Because the one you are now with can see what you did previously and they may think about you poorly as someone with a history of fake relationships. It does say a lot about you. People always have the story that I was young.

Well, we all passed by there to get to the age we are today, but where was the common sense in doing any of it? There are some things we do in our life that come and go, and others follow us all our lives. I think that there is no hiding from them, and I feel as if tattoos are one of them. And when you are a lady of the streets or man as well, your mistakes follow you as well. For one, you never truly trust your past even if you call yourself cleaned up now, you battle with yourself, and the lack of trust shows in your actions because the person that you were with wasn't like you?

Some aren't wise enough to realize what the problem is in your relationship, but the ones on the outside can see clearly what's really going on. They know they can't reach you, and they will hold it to themselves from you, but share it with others about you. I don't know if I would call them true friends because I would feel like I should be able to come to you with an understanding heart and mind for you, but as I might listen, let's say I'm no better than your other so-called friends because I'm not saying anything either. That's when two wrongs don't make any right in the situation at all, and the hurt and pain are written all over your face, but you're still trying to hang in there.

However, all the people on the outside are just looking in, but you're in there for the long run, and that's truly an act of God in you; because if it were me, I would have left a long time ago, and there was nothing anyone could have told me to make me stay. Maybe this was another one of my downfalls in life. I used to be a great runner, but today, I don't even want to start playing the game. I'm happy right where I'm at, and the stupid stuff can miss me altogether.

I've seen the game, and the faces just change, but the game remains the same. The game is so widespread that the players are as young as twelve years old today. They don't care who they play either. The game is so strong, and they sold it to the ones they shouldn't have which is themselves. They believe it, and that's sad. I met a guy who has lived a jail bird's life, but he is out now.

I never believe all the stuff that he says because as he opened his mouth to me, I could see where he was coming from, which was nowhere. Nothing that he told me I believed, and he wanted me to think he had money, yet I knew he was always looking for a handout and not a hand up. I laughed on the inside but did speak out because I just couldn't let him think he was making a fool out of me.

He was an old player, and as soon as he started talking, I could hear my father telling me to watch out for cats just like him. I did the first thing and took a good look at him. I dressed him with my eyes from head to toe. He wanted me to think he was a millionaire, yet he looked like fifteen cents at best. He was bragging on stuff as if he was reading a script in a play, so I figured out how he got on with the girl he was with; he fed her the stupid stuff and being much younger than him, he read the script that he practiced so well and sold it to himself first. Of course, he bought it as well, and she went for it listening to him, and not knowing what to truly look out for in men. We all have passed this road in life in one way or another. The people, the places, or things that just wasn't good for us.

It's no shortcoming on her behalf but his own. He rolled out the red carpet, and she walked down it open-hearted and fell for it. Well, I wasn't her and wasn't buying any of it, and once he realized he wasn't talking to no fool, he shut up talking to me because I called his bluff for sure. And he couldn't back up anything that he had put out, none of it at all, and he knew it as well, and you honestly could have heard a pin drop.

It's sad because people walk around daily, doing this same old game. I believe that different faces and the former players should have grown up by now, but they haven't; not at all, as they are still trying to run the really stupid stuff in this day and time. Well for me, it's just ain't working, and for me, it wasn't working forty years ago. That's because I had a daddy for one and a real father for two, but most of all he was a real man, and that's what kept his daughters (including me) half-way straight. Oh, we did stuff like anyone else might have, which our parents might not like or respect as well. However, we were raised to know the difference, and if we choose to do wrong, then that was on us.

God prepares us for our walk in Him as well, and when we choose to do otherwise, then that's on us. It does not happen because the road hadn't been laid out for us but because we choose to do differently, and that's when the free will of God kicks in our lives. Again, God wants more for us than we want for ourselves. Then the saddest part is that some people sit in the church all their lives for whatever reason, but never get the glory of God and the will of God for them within their lives.

And that's sad as they may go to hell through the church, out of all the places the world. These people are surely churchgoers, and some of them never miss a service, but they never sincerely become a Christian because they never added Christ into their lives for real. They always ran behind whoever they made their God.

I'm not the man chaser, not at all but seek the kingdom of God and all of His righteousness. People get mad at me because I choose not to buy into what they are trying to sell me. I always feel like, they aren't going to get up and go to work for me in the morning, and they aren't the ones I pray to at night to let me get up and go to work; so how can they tell me what to do with my money?

They indeed think I'm crazy, but I don't care because they have no control over me, and I'm not as mad as they might think. I believe that they are crazy for thinking they are fooling me. Sometimes when one is not saying anything, it's not because they don't know any better, it's because they know that you don't know any better.

At the end of the day, only one of us is mad or upset, and it's not me, so guess who's left, you! You'll be mad at me as I have money in my pocket, but I am not willing to give the same to become money in your pocket, where you're trying to get it with one thing or another all the time. If we ain't talking about money, then we ain't talking at all, and when I don't turn it over, you're very disrespectful to me, and I can live with that! I had someone today ask me three hundred dollars for some reason. Now before they asked, I had let them talk about me, of all people. They told me I was harder than a rock or mountain. Then they said, the only thing that could break the mountain or rock was steel. Then they said, you're harder than steel. Then they asked me for three hundred dollars, and when I said, I don't have three hundred dollars to give away today, they judged my salvation. If I had all the monies that they stole from me and pawned my stuff as the list goes on, and if I had found any good in them, things might have been different, but since I haven't the answer is no!

God has given me the wisdom to know the difference in people action and what they truly stand for and therefore I'm good at all times within my life and when they tell me what I can afford, let's say it seems funny to me. As amusing as it can be, and sometimes when I'm alone and think about some of the stuff they may have said, I just bust out laughing because laughing is good for my soul when it's due to others who think they are making a fool out of me. This young lady who has been working with me made a statement that no two days are the same at this store, and she finds me funny.

Well, no two days are the same anywhere in the world. Every new day that God gives to us is a new beginning in Him. Things of yesterday are pasted with the fresh morning dew, and the brightness of the day begins. It takes out yesterday and brings in today with a fresh perspective. We can make it good or bad or with our choices and efforts. All of that depends on us what we do when God allows us to see the day. It's as good or bad as we make it and it's truly us. God gave it to us, and what we do with it is up to us.

Some people wake up thinking who they will set out to rob or steal from today. Others wake up wanting to be a blessing to someone today, that's truly me. My mind stays on the Mercy God has placed in my life. And the praises are in my mouth for the mercy of him, and anybody that knows me can understand what I do.

Saying that she really doesn't know me nor understand just how good is to me. She is just like this guy, who walks around mentally unbalanced. If you offer him a job, he finds a reason for not doing it. Yet, he is always looking for a handout and bragging that he's a man. I beg the difference. I've been lucky to have had some great men in my family. I have also had the pleasure to work around men and service many of them who bring much value within their lives as well. But this cat, he's something else, and I made it a point to point out to her girl with the people who come in the door that truly do know me. She has a weird look on her face, not truly understanding, but I say it's because she's young. Being young isn't always the answer to the things going on around you, but it sounds good to keep it moving. Young people have more today than ever, but they don't get the essential things in life. Hand them a phone or computer, and they understood how to use that, but throw everyday little stuff at them, and they don't get it.

It drives me crazy trying to make them get it, so the easy way out is to let these sleepy dogs lay as they like. I know that's selfish! This is true but coming back from the dead makes me see and do things so differently now, and I can't let them stress me out over the smallest stuff. I know it will get to me, and I'm not trying to go through anything else, so please forgive me, but I'm just not with it anymore. Over the years all the people that I decided to help, well let's say, I didn't help them nor me. So today,

I'm letting God do the impossible because I may want it for them, but they don't want it for themselves.

Heartache and Pain

I had a friend call me with a lot on her plate this week. And all I can say is the devil is trying to get busy within her life again, and she's letting him do it. Who does the devil use the most? Your children, your spouse, and any family member that he can! And what do you do? You let him because you get so caught up with foolishness that it's unreal. You don't listen to what anybody or I have to say to you.

How could you call me for advice and not respect what I'm trying to tell you for your own good? You're not listening, and the devil is rejoicing over your stubbornness. He only wants the bad for you, and you're falling for the trick of our mortal enemy. He has you right where he wants you to be. You are locked down in the sin ties that he lays for you to fall open-heartedly in, and you ran straight to him with no problem. Well, sometimes we get so worked up with things going on in our family or friends that we miss the true picture. It's all out of God's blessing from the beginning, and you can't make it right but get more messed up than anything. Sometimes you must just stay back and see what the devil has done to your life. You may have been helping him and must learn to understand it yourself. You call, and I would go off running from you to avoid problems. Not today, I'm not jumping for anybody's mess, regardless of who they think they are.

They're not getting me caught up because I have no power in my hand but have to do what they should be doing, taking it to Jesus, and leaving it in His hands as He is the only one who can make a difference in your life. If you really know God, then you know when to stand still and wait on the only one who can heal and release the daily stress within one's life. He is always standing there waiting on you, but you are never waiting on Him.

There is nothing too hard for God, and He and He alone never fails us. Others will come and go within our lives, but God will always be a prayer away and provide all our needs according to His will for our life. When you are in doubt, pray, and when you question, pray, and when you reach anything that you think is too hard for you, then give it straight to the Number One healer in your life, God! He's good, and nothing is beyond Him. God is good at all times in one's life, and no one can tell me anything else because I know God is good for myself.

My healing and wellbeing is my testimony of the mercy of God, within all times in my life for the mercy of God has always restored me, and all I can say is, God is great! And what I know about Jesus, He's alright with me too. I can't thank Him enough for restoring my life, and the praises will always flow out of my mouth to the glory of God because that's all that I have in my life to stand on. Everything else that I've tried has failed me in so many ways.

I just could never tell it all, and some of the people, who misused me; still today, try to get me to trust them again. But I indeed know better than to do it again, but that doesn't stop me from showing kindness, in so many small ways. That's the love of God within my heart, but I'm never to trust a relationship with these people either. When we put our trust in people, sometimes it doesn't take long to find out who they indeed are.

My friend had gotten caught up with a con artist. Well, I saw that because little did she know how many times I've run into such con artists myself in the past. If I could have stopped her from the road that she took, I would have; but sometimes people have to go through things for themselves to truly learn from it. Oh, but once you know, you shouldn't allow yourself to go back for any more of these scams. We should always learn from our shortcomings, in order to have real growth.

And when God speaks to us in His soft voice to warn us, we should be listening to him for our own good in our lives. Sad to say, but we don't ever listen to God; we only hear him after it is too late. As I have done so many times within my own life, and it's sad, but I'm just starting to listen more now than ever before.

Here is an example of my learning. Well, this man laid out the tightest game before me, using God as his main line to catch me off-guard. Yet I told him, that God didn't say it because God didn't show it to you and me both. I must say that I've seen this game played before that he was putting in front of me. Just when he started to tell me of all people, what God told him, I said, I knew that all he was saying was wrong about me. I allowed him to talk, and I took it with a smile of kindness because first of all God knows better and secondly, I knew better as well. He can lie to a man and fool him, but he can't lie to God and deceive Him.

"For all have sinned, and come short of the glory of God; 24) Being justified freely by his grace through the redemption that is in Christ Je'-sus: 25) Whom God hath set forth to be a propitiation through faith in his blood, to declare his righteousness for the remission of sins that are past, through for the forbearance of God; 26) To declare, I say, at this time his righteousness: that he might be just, and justifier of him which believeth in Je'-sus. 27) Where is boasting then? It is excluded. By what law? of works? Nay; but by the law of faith"

-Romans 3: 23-27

We are always walking by faith and not by our sight, which is limited. Things don't ever look like what they are in real at any time within our lives. We always have more than we are ever looking for, which is going on within our lives every day, and then things are never as they seem when we look in anyone's life. God has always wanted more for us than we want for ourselves. Through our faith, we gain redemption for our sins and righteousness; thereafter, we find it in Christ as He strengthens us. Sometimes, there is nothing that we can justify in our lives because we never looked at the glass as half full and were always trying to fill it up to its maximum.

When we find it is not, we feel that there is no growth within our lives. Yesterday, a friend told me that I should have had my house built the way I wanted it from the start. While I felt she didn't like my answer to her about my home. First of all, I picked the lot. Then I picked the style that I had wanted. Then I put in it what I wanted at that time. But now I'm redoing it because I like change and there is nothing wrong with that. I feel that since I get up and go to work each day, six days a week, I should be able to have anything that I want the way that I want it to be, anytime I feel like it.

If I like to change things for me, that's okay, and if you like your stuff to stay the same, then that's okay for you. Nothing that I do in my home cost anyone but me. Anyway, I was lost but kept it moving anyway. Then I figured the Mercy of God within her life hasn't grown enough to understand it. She does all the stuff that she does on a man like clockwork, but always I run on the mercy and blessing of God, and that's different. People don't truly understand grace and mercy because they haven't arrived at that point in their lives yet.

What they might say or do, I could sit and try to bring it to them, yet I don't; mainly because they think they are smarter than me, and I don't mind. When I look at how they live now and have lived their entire lives, I come out smelling like a rose. Let's not forget that there's no big or little sin to God. It's all the same, but we don't think so because we judge things differently. I have never been one to drink alcohol or just go out there in the streets but used to put me up better than the ones that people call hoes and drunks, and the list goes on.

I do give myself better credit than them, and I know in God's eyes, I'm still no better than them, but certainly have less to repent for. Some of them don't repent at all and act as if it didn't matter because God forgives them for their shortcomings but when you never correct your sins, then what is the purpose of going in and out of church every few days? That's why when they tell me they are a Christian, I look for the message of God in them. I can't find it, so on that note, I flee from them at every chance I get.

Whose mouth is full of cursing and bitterness: 15) Their feet are swift to shed blood: 16) Destruction and misery are in their ways: And the way of peace have they not know: 18) There is no fear of God before their eyes. 19) Now we know that what things soever the law saint, it saith to them who are under the law: that every mouth may be stopped, and all the world may become guilty before God.

-Romans 3: 14-19

In all things we will stand before God one day. How we stand before him matters greatly in our lives. The good things that one might say they were doing just may not cut it because He wasn't in it. I call it the big show by fake people. They put it on every week, never truly living anything unto God at all.

They buy the big flowers, nice balloons, and enjoy excellent dinners as well, but only what they do for Christ will count for them, not the ones that you might be trying to impress. I say, keep my name out of your mouth for a good reason because if God did it, He and He alone will reward me for it.

It's that simple, and He blesses me daily for my reward starts when I got up this morning and enjoyed the abundance of life all day long unto Him. So when people say: I talk too much, they aren't lying, but as long as it has a purpose and brings value to one's life, then I've done the work of God. He can use me as likes according to His will for my life each day. Some days it's all about me, and others it's all about someone else, I don't even know, but it's always a blessing of God's mercy, keeping us pushing forward within our lives.

I had my annual Fourth of July cookout for my customers, who had no one to spend the holiday with. Well, it was horribly done this year, and it wasn't my fault, but I did a lot of praying to get beyond the day. I won't go into details about it but let's say, it took a lot of prayers, and I'm not over it yet. When you put your heart into something, you only look for the best in what you do, but then it does not always turn out perfectly which hurts you if you are not careful. This was July the 1st for me this year. God's mercy had my back in favor of all things, especially today.

We have times when we look at people and trust them, and then they aren't honest with us. Well, this is one of those times. My friend of more than thirty years let me down in this incident. Now we have worked together in the past and done stuff like that, but this was truly a disappointment that I never faced before. He knew that he had done something wrong, and he didn't fix it but continue to move forward as if the problem would just go away. The issue at this point could have been worse than it was, but thanks to God it wasn't.

Again favor is fair if you're serving Jesus at all times, within one's life. Believe me, this was one of those times for me. I had been warned before, but yet I continued to trust him. But this time, it could have been a life or death chance for me. And there would not have been anything that I could have said to fix the situation. I can't truly go into it because for one, the pain of the day is still written all over my face and the hurt in my heart is still burning. And I now cannot trust this man because if it would have been me, let's say I would have done it right for peace' sake at any cost to me.

The welfare of others is too vital for me, and everyone doesn't take things the same, and for me, I don't know why! They should look out for others as they would want to be treated themselves, but this isn't always true as in most cases, people don't apply the grace and mercy of God in their actions. I did because the love of people in my heart was the plan for the day. I don't just think about me anymore, but all the ones around me and wish others do the same, especially when it comes to thinking about what you do and who will be affected by the choices that you make. If we all did that, what a wonderful world this would be! Then and only then can the true love of God be shown within one's life, like a bright light that's forever burning. God's plan for us is always great. If we listen to him when we get in a tight corner like I did this weekend, we must turn to him for favor and guidance along the way. God had me once again in His hand with much favor for me. I can't ever thank God enough for all the blessing of Him. He is the one who bestows me with all the wisdom and knowledge.

He and He alone finds me worthy within His eyesight. The God that I'm talking about is the same true God we all should be servings at all times in our lives. Whether things are good or bad, it doesn't matter, but we should still give Him the utmost praise; not just for good but for the seemingly ugly too. This was an unpleasant event for me. But God got the praise within it. This was truly painful, I just couldn't pray enough. This was heartbreaking, yet I'll serve him in the storm of the event of the day, and if it could have gone wrong today, I would still found the glory of God after the rain. And it really rained today as well but only for a moment. My heart was raining all day until I went to bed.

I really couldn't get a really good night sleep because some people took Uber to my house, yet Uber is not a service available where I live, so they had to spend the night. That was the smallest of my problems because I had room for them. But then some others came late, and I was upset because people carried all the food home, and others showed up without anything left to eat.

No one really played games, not even the children so the fellowship wasn't good at all and that was the least of my problems. I'm not going to stop the event, but I will change the people that I invite to my events to make it more successful because everyone in my current list isn't a team player but team hater. When they drink hater-aid, they should be drinking Kool-Aid which is a better drink. Today, you can control your sweetest in the drink. That was something to grow on from me, and I'm saying: just do it, but do it right so you can get some glory and mercy out of it. God still provides glory at the end. And if nothing else, peace is still present in favor of God.

(For that righteous man dwelling among them, in seeing and hearing, vexed his righteous soul from day

*to day with their unlawful deeds;) 9) The Lord knoweth
how to deliver the godly out of temptations, and to
reserve the unjust unto the day of judgment to be
punished: 10) But chiefly them that walk after the flesh
in the lust of uncleanness, and despise government.
Presumptuous are they, selfwilled, they are not afraid
to speak evil of dignities. 11) Whereas angels, which
are greater in power and might, bring not railing
accusation against them before the Lord. 12) But these,
as natural brute beasts, made to be taken and
destroyed, speak evil of the things that they understand
not; and shall utterly perish in their own corruption;
13) And shall receive the reward of unrighteousness, as
they that count it pleasure to riot in the day time. Spots
they are blemishes, sporting themselves with their own
deceivings while they feast with you.*

-Peter 2: 8-13

It is funny that what looks bad sometimes becomes a blessing unto you for your good, and God still gets the glory at the end of the day. My day didn't start out as well as I had planned it nor was it what I had planned for it to end up like; yet, God had a better plan in his hands for me. My cousins had come from Kentucky for my event. Well, I had other ideas on my mind, and I had plenty of things that I wanted to do with them, yet God had a better plan for all of us. They were my biggest supporters for the event. Not that my daughter and her friend didn't do a lot because she helped cook while her friend took care of all the odds and ins for me.

They opened my eyes up truly. Sometimes, it is difficult for us to handle everything. It is better to move over and let someone else handle things for you. Well, that's what I will do for my next event. Let someone else control it and relax and enjoy with the guests that come out. I honestly never did that as I always became so busy trying to run stuff and cook a lot of the food as well. It meant that I really never enjoyed any of it, and then when things don't go as they should, I faced problems! And I don't like challenges, and I'm sure that no one else does either, but definitely not me when I shouldn't have had them in the beginning.

It's a new day, and I have learned a brighter way of doing things for sure. Christmas is coming, and I will then host my next event. I'm looking for a sunny day in Christ for one, as it's all about Him. Then again I also want it to be a glorious day in the Lord, for He and He alone is worthy. I'm beginning to start planning for success now. I won't let anything steal my joy. Within everything we do, we should get something from it. I stopped looking for people who think and do things like me. And the word of God said: trust no man! He was talking about mankind. The flesh is always weak and allow us to do some crazy stuff within one's life, mostly not thinking about the outcome?

So we move forward without thinking about the true outcome of what we might be doing. I've learned if I got to go down, I'm going by myself, but I am not trusting anyone to pull me down with them. It's not how long you have known anyone today but where they are mentally and physically with you. They could call themselves helping, but it's not always in your favor as for me in this case. Not that I think it was being mean or anything.

However, they knew better, but they still made a mess out of my event. Then sometimes you got to look at age, and my friend is 86 years of age. So, I feel that time has not been on his side as he can't do things that he used to do any longer, and it's just not working in his favor anymore. Still, I know his heart meant good, but things just didn't turn out that way. This happens to all of us;

and some don't get to even 50 years old, and things start to fall apart for them. I remember that things got really crazy when I was about 45 years old. I guess when the big ball hit me, and I'm just now getting it right again or should I say what I feel is getting it right now.

Time tells all stories within one's life and, with the guidance of God, some of us go back and put our life back together again. I feel that's where I am now, on the track of resurrection in my life. When we take time to get things back on track, we indeed win in the game called life, but sometimes people never get it right again nor even try to change. They get stuck where they are and don't even try, and that's sad. I'm too strong for that. You can knock me down, but I won't stay down for long. You can block my way, but I'm the one who will try to push my way through you.

Will power is the greatest power in the world. It begins mentally before we take any physical action. So a man thinks, so he is. And if you think you can, you will, and if you think you can't, you never will. Thinking and giving in to God brings His power alive within one's life and offers them His mercy. No God, no growth! To gain knowledge, you must grow daily in Him. It's that simple, at least for me. I can't tell nobody how to live, but I can tell you my stories as I walk in the anointing of God within my life, and know the healing and blessing of him for myself. I pray for the grace, mercy, and anointing to fall down within everyone's life from Christ the same way as for me, but we all know everybody isn't seeking him in the same manner.

Some people are speaking it, but they aren't living anything close to the words of God. They were not called by God, and you must watch out for them. They dress for the part and speak the words of God as well, yet they aren't living what they are speaking or preaching. They are the false prophets that the word of God speaks on in many places.

Their game has gotten stronger, and the presence of them sounds and looks good. But it's always about them and never about the people of God, and you must ask God for wisdom and mercy to know the difference, and He will show you everything. I have faced some strong issues in my life. I've trusted people based on what they said they were until I went back to Jesus for guidance and asked him to show me and He did. Be careful of things that you want to be answered by God. You can receive results for which you may not be prepared to handle. In some cases, be careful what you're praying for and make sure you can handle it.

God sometimes gives us things that He knows aren't good for us, but He does it anyway, and even when we don't have a clue about what we are praying for, God grants it, and when it's a mess, he cleans it up again and again for us. This is since He doesn't quit on us, but we quit on Him even with the slightest problem. Then, when we get our act together, well let's say God moves in a mighty way within our lives.

Things will always happen to us, but grace and mercy will always keep us pushing forward in Christ. I stopped by one of my sisters' house on my way to the doctor. Well, I was talking about a statement that one of my kids made to me about how many husbands I have had. The key word was "*husbands*". So I've been married as many times as the days of the week since God respects marriage. But to say that you change men more than her and my other sisters, wow! They have had more boyfriends than I've had husbands. Although one has never been married which is true, their track record speaks for itself because if you change sheets without a commitment from men, you're out of God's will for our lives. Oh, I do know that all marriages aren't what God wanted for me either, so I only had it half right in my life. There was no commitment in the relationship, so God wasn't present in it either. This is one of those glasses that was half full but not half empty.

To fill it up I would have had to have a commitment to the relationship and that thing *for better or worse, and in sickness and in health, and to death do us part* would have had to be in there as well, and I've never had any of this in me. Today, I'm good and all by myself. I've found that if I can't be happy with you then, I could be happy without you. God in one's life is all you'll ever need. I've had a man sprinkle a lie that he didn't ask me to marry him.

Well, who makes up something so stupid about anyone? If he had not asked, then I would not have said so, it's that simple. I know that he's living with someone else. Now that's fine with me because the shortcomings are within him and not in me. When you find God for real, then He becomes the man and solution for every moment in your life. He's your pillow to cry on and the joy in the morning when you wake up, and that glory within your walk past the mirror. There's no end to God within one's life at any time when you learn to serve Him to attain His mercy.

Make every day as having your glass half full and allow God to keep it full with an overflow from Him. The roads get shorter, the load gets lighter, the peace of mind kicks in, and you get the glory of everything in your life. Then and only then, no devil in earth or any spirit of Satan can destroy your life for you have learned how to hear and don't hear, and see and don't see.

And as the devil is moving, you start praying for deliverance from that spirit and keep moving in the spirit of God because you know who you are and who they are as well, and then that becomes more than enough for you. Now life is worth living all because of the God in you, and your serving shows in His eyes even if no one else notices it. It's funny how someone can tell you about yourself but never stop to see their own shortcoming because they don't think they have any. I say clean out your backyard before you attempt to pull trash in mine. They are so perfect on their way to hell in the gasoline draws that they are wearing and serving Satan when meanwhile they are giving you what! Nothing of any good for anyone, not even them? So they spend their whole life not ever truly growing in most areas.

The money they make may look useful to them. The house looks good as well, but their soul out of all things does not look good because there is no God in anything they do in their life, nothing at all. That's sad for them and even more depressing when they go to church, but Christ is never playing a role within their life, and they will miss heaven on their way to hell by means of the church out of all places, and they can't see that it's not okay with Jesus.

All I want is a little more Jesus in my life. For He is truly what I need to make my life complete, and that's enough for me. When you have been through so much heartbreak and pain in your life, you have to find comfort within God and His mercy within your life daily. He will become everything for you, and His Mercy will keep you from falling too far out of the arms of God; you will learn how worthy you truly are when you remain close to Him. Keep faith and your chin up because you will make it! It's the promise of God on our life, and His purpose is to place His favor for us. The word of God becomes real when we really trust it and apply it to our lives.

Happiness comes from one's self. I have become selfish in so many ways. I found the things that I once thought I was doing right were so wrong for me, and they weren't benefiting anyone, not even myself. I ripped and ran, and at the end of the day, I was tired for nothing.

And the same people that I tried to help robbed and took anything of any value that they needed from me without a single thought of what it was going to do to me. Then God opened up my spiritual eyes unto people, places, and things daily. Then and only then the light went on, and I began to change.

Change is always hard to make because at first, you're happy with how you are and think you are perfect. You believe everyone's wrong and you're right. And when you don't find fault in you, you don't grow. When you're not looking for help, then you don't need it. And then, as they say, two wrongs don't make one right. Oh, that's so true too because I've lived trying to make that work as well. And so, I don't drink or party or any odd stuff, but I'm still far from being perfect because as I said before, sometimes I'm selfish. And right now is one of those times. I like saying when I eat, my whole family has eaten, and I don't have anyone to take care of them but myself.

But just because I feel that way, that doesn't make it right. My kids think it's so wrong because I don't want to help them, but I think differently. I feel all burned out, and say if I was dead, then what would you do? Well, act like it and do it like I'm not here. I know how selfish that may sound and how far out of God it may be to some eyes, but after the stuff I've been through, the pain is still alive in many things, and I'm not entirely delivered either.

I know God is not finished with me yet, and it's a lifelong growing process. We sometimes think since we have accepted Christ, everything is alright. Well, that's not true. We remain a big piece of work as living like Christ is the hardest thing you will ever have to do in your life. Keeping him first before you do anything else is always hard; to think and act like Christ isn't easy. Then to live a Christian life before Christ and society is also hard because Christ is not judging you but men will. He overlooks your faults and sees the good in you, but people don't. He lets go and forgives, but men, again never do that, although they never look at their vices. How quickly can one overlook themselves, but see everything wrong with you? How strange that sounds but so true! God giveth, and only God can take things away.

Whether good or bad, he has full control. To feel if your efforts make you grow in life, you can't sit with the same people. You can't hang with them either because they don't see or want what you're looking for from God, so they can't understand nor want anything good for you as well. I know there are times that I have wanted more for people that they wanted for themselves. But when you see that spirit in them, you must learn to say no. Not because you don't want to help them, but to make them apply themselves for the things they want the most. If you need a handout, don't talk to me, but if you want a hand up, then I'm there for you.

This isn't valid just on the streets but in the church as well. I get tired of the church game and some places that I go; all that that they want is to play a money game, and when you're not playing, then they aren't speaking to you. The calls stop, and the handshakes quickly go away too, and when they see you, they quickly run the other way. None of this is God, not at all. But it's today's churchgoers, and I run from them as well; I don't want that evil spirit in them to fall on me. It's funny because it begins with the head, and they are the same way, so it must be true that people run behind the ones that live and look like them as well.

I can see them for who they truly are, and God is not in it at all. My saying is that birds of a feather flock together because they all hold and share the same sin tie secrets among them as well. When you look around and see things like they are shacking up with one woman, then they have kids with two or more members and sleeping with even more. They can't let them leave because of the ties that they have on them from one week to the next, and you see it; when you don't know it's one thing, but when you learn, that's something different.

You don't tell, and I won't say anything because we're all in it together. And you know they can't drag you down without pulling themselves down as well. So things go on the same pattern business as usual, but God ain't in it at all. I get a laugh out of it because I think they believe they are in the Bible days, with the concubines and so much more, but what God had to say about it was that it's out of order! But today, people are still trying to live as such, and who are they leading? They want you if you're not careful.

Then they stay or leave the church, well that's a big no because you can't let them go, for the things you are doing out of order might get out, so you do everything that you can to keep them happy because you know if you don't the outcome will not be pleasant for you and the church that's already in pieces. You can't get it right or put it back together again, no matter how hard you might be trying, but the main thing you need is what you don't have in life, and that's Jesus; for He and He alone can restore the sin that has fallen all over the church. Well, if you know what you're looking at first hand, then you know it for what it is and what you're sitting there.

You often watch it unfolding before your eyes as well. When you see it, you wonder how you got there in the first place. Well, that was me, and I realize now how I got there. It was true that someone fed me stuff to get me there in the first place. Well, God didn't lead me there as He has protected me while I was sitting there. He allowed me to see but didn't say anything.

He allowed me to pray for the things that I saw but couldn't change. When I did speak out about what I was raised in, the true way that I believed to be the correct way of serving in God's eyesight, and the commitment of serving God kicked in my life, and all that I was taught as a child to take place in my life.

The Bible says: raise a child, the way it's to go, and when they get old, they won't depart from it. So when I see things, I do know the difference, and the spirit of God's teaching and learning will kick into the kid's life. When we are taught and trained with the true ways of living and serving God, we can hope to do well. When you know who you are and then who you are serving, God removes the ungodliness that you may run across in your life.

That's when you truly take that next shift in Christ that moves you to a higher level with Him as offering your salvation in him. God again will lead you and guide you within him, if we are listening, and He will show you who they are and who they are not in him as well. The complete word of God is the truth, and everyone else is a liar, and shall not, and will not prosper unto God for everything that they may try to do will always fail and come falling down. Some get away for many of years, but they too come falling down slowly but surely, as time passes.

They say what is done in the dark comes to light, and no one can't hide that no matter how hard they try. Then when they learn who you are, they flee from you because they realize that you're not who they thought you were, and those devils will escape from the God's grace and mercy in you. They get speechless and can't even talk to you, and when they see you, they run the other way! This is the power of God moving in your life; believe that, and He knows that they can't handle the truth nor the walk of God in you, so they flee and flee quickly.

The God we serve protects us at all times in all situations and ways in one's life when we commit ourselves unto him in all things and especially the so-called church or house of God. For it to be indeed a house of God, he must dwell between the walls. I have been to places and walked out of the stronghold that I felt wasn't present there correctly.

Also, I've been to places where it felt like I was the only one genuinely serving and knowing the works of God for His subjects. This statement is so hardcore because I'm sure some of the people were interested in finding God, but in what way because they looked at me as if they didn't understand the words that came out of my mouth about God.

They cannot understand the healing and blessing of him, or there was no anointing of Him in the handshake. Then they cannot understand my praise too because they question it, and I wondered to myself, why didn't they truly know God for themselves? I wondered where they were in Christ themselves. We were both lost. When you take things to God, he gives a new understanding of all things; that's the renewing of one's mind about whatever is going on in one's life. That's in scripture or everyday living. God doesn't gossip, not at all; but gives understanding to people, and He gives you what you just experience in the close of the day that you're bringing to him. He makes the things you can't understand plain unto you mind, so you don't get misled. He keeps you on track with Him and not lost among other misguided souls. The game of life is like everything else in the world; there are two sides to everything.

There's a right and a wrong, a stop and go, a cute and ugly, and a high and low, and a good and bad. The choices we make, create the difference in our lives. If we know better, we should do better too. To know and not do, is all on us. To make excuses to cover up our wrongdoing and to justify it is totally out of God, but we do it.

And it sounds good when you say God understands and He forgives me, so you can keep up the mess that you're happily living in any way. Well, you better get beyond that scripture and recalibrate the roads that you are living and traveling on, within your life and where it's going to end up. If you don't make the necessary shift changes in your life, then you're going to end up in the pits of hell. If you believe that someone else is leading you toward this path, you will find them as your partners present in hell with you as well. I had a talk with someone who was trying to sell themselves to me. Well, when you truly know people for who they are, and they freely lie all the time in everything they do, they expose themselves. They are standing on a pool pit or the ground. You know them so well that you know they aren't going to do anything they say.

You can pretty much know what to expect from them as well. This can include people who are the closest to you. It often includes your family members and life partner. It may even be your pastor who's supposed to be a leader but has no such thing in him as keeping the matter between God and them and you.

They can't wait to tell it to whoever will listen and when you hear it again, you don't even know it anymore. Wow, who does that? The ones you put your faith and trust into but had no good for you at heart from the beginning. You trusted them anyway because you didn't honestly know who they were. I've learned to give it all to Jesus, and He won't say one word but send the little child of God to your rescue, and you're left wondering where they came from, out of the blue to help you. Well, this has happened to me more times in the last ten years than I can count. God sent his best to me in trying times in my life. Things began to happen that I too didn't understand, but I had to go back and give God praise for his grace that he put in my path, and the mercy that was shared over my life.

Sometimes I didn't have much money to pay the phone bill, but God sent someone in to hand it to me. I didn't have rent money but someone called and told me they had money that they needed to spend and get out of their budget before the week was over, and they needed a backdated invoice to give it to me.

But the ones that I've had so much trust and faith inlet me down until they needed something else, and that's when they came knocking at my door or ringing on my phone. I moved on from that because they constitute what was holding me down in the first place. When you realize who they are and what impact they have already had on your life, you got to make the shift change in life for the good of you. If you don't, they will keep pulling you down with them, and that's your fault and not theirs because the devil knows who you are and he will use anybody close to you to keep holds on you. He comes to kill and steal and destroy you from within anyway that he can, but he doesn't win, if you don't let him. So you must cut negative people in your life away with the love of God in your heart.

These are people who have no good for you in their hearts, and you've seen what a better day of your life will bring for you. They are doing what the devil would have them do, and they don't understand you at all because they're not where you are in Christ; so they can't understand, and they say you're crazy. Yes, crazy about that man called Jesus, and no other man is worth my salvation.

They will come and go, and they will try you even with a title and robe, but you better know where you stand and remain firm on the words of God. That's more than enough for you because he's the man that will never fail you nor leave you nor let you down and will always be right there for the asking. I assure you that you can take all your problems to Him, and you can leave them there. He won't tell a soul, and you don't ever have anything to ever worry about with Him on your side. Oh, how wonderful life becomes with Christ. All the glory and grace lives in Him and then you as you serve Him, you receive it in your life. God wrote what He wanted from all of us in His word, and I also wrote what I wanted from God. He released many things unto me a day at a time. The Bible is our guideline to life every day. For we must use it to our advantage daily to receive the blessing that God has for our lives.

That's the true power of prayer, and that's when I see people who say they know God, and they say they are serving God. I find that although they say they were called, I never see the growth of Christ in their life. God says you will know the spirit, and that's why they can't take me anyway with them because the spirit of Christ just isn't there, and I'm not joining them on that path to nowhere.

They aren't going anywhere fast but to hell in their messes that they sat fourth within their life while God had nothing to do with any of it. You would think they would want to get it right, but they don't because they are so happy doing and living like they do within their wrongdoings, and God will have the last words if they don't get it right before it's too late. Then and only then will they realize who God is, and what he can truly do within one's life! But only if it's not too late for them already.

8) Will a man rob God? Yet he have robbed me. But he say, Wherein have we robbed thee? In tithes and offerings. Well, tithes and offerings aren't always a thing about what money one has in his pocket? It can be your stewardship in the things that you do for Christ, not the money you put in church but today all they want is money, and the salvation of the Lord is last on their list. Then time unto God is something else.

When you take time out of your daily task and make time for others, then it's an offering unto the Lord making time for his people of God, and that replaces all the money in the world. God loves outshine all things unto him in so many small ways, and when they rob God, it's your giving that you sowed into the ministries that they use ungodly not what you did but what they did.

9) Ye are cursed with a curse' for ye have robbed me, even this whole nation. The world is cursed with the sin ties of the fault profits of the world, and there is no getting around the things that they preach and teach worldwide. They are on the television and the internet and everywhere that you may watch, and if you sit and listen to them one by one you'll find that they are not on one accord as ministries should be.

If God was indeed the head, then they would be on one accord in him. That's who God is, a unity. The big money is what preachers are after. They come together in the things that they do and price out what we're pulling in on this event, and what they're going to pull in. They count you in the sales of the tickets first. Then the ones that might come to the door and the sale of books and CDs and tee shirts, and the list goes on, but the poor chase them looking for prosperity in them instead of favor of God.

The Bible says: the poor will be with us always. They make millions and the ones helping them stay right where they are until they find God for themselves. The lines start out at one thousand dollars, and then they keep going down. When you go back and add up the amount that they just raised you would be surprised. I've seen the case when they took up twenty thousand or more in the line before they're asked the rest of the people to give.

When all totals are added up, and they say, you're giving it to help the people less fortunate than you, but they never see it happen, ever. The poor will be with us always, so the word of God says. And so will those who lie and steal and do other ungodly things. They sit all around and over us if we are looking closely at them. The houses never get too big and the cars never too much, and you sit in that same old house and driving that same old car and continuing to say you're looking for your blessing from the Lord. Now I think you're crazy for listening to all that foolishness. I see some keep running, and when I am talking about the healing and blessing of God, they got to go?

I'm not going to stop talking, but they are welcome to always stop listening. When the nerves hit home, and

55

*I'm not on the phone, they are still thinking about what
I had to say, so who are they kidding? Let's see, only
themselves.*

*10) Bring he all the tithes into the storehouse, that there
may be meat in mine house, and prove me now
herewith, saith the Lord of hosts, if I will not open up
the windows of heaven, and pour you out a blessing,
that there shall not be room enough to receive it.*

-Malachi 3: 8-10 with explanations

Chapter 2
My Glorified Events

God continues to want more for us than we want for ourselves. He gives freely unto the ones sowing seed for his name's sake. I take twice a year and give back to the ones that were there for me. I say if you don't have anyone to spend the Fourth of July with, then come eat at my table and then the same thing goes for Christmas dinner. Well, this is my offering unto God's people. Some come with an open heart and others come just to have their nose in someone else's business.

Then the devil never misses a time to come and destroy something if he could. He doesn't get much joy or pleasure out of my events. The people that come, for the most part, have the spirit of God shown to me. I don't invite the ones that I feel I would make uncomfortable in my home. Mainly because I don't smoke or drink and things like that, and I wouldn't want them to feel out of place at my house because I don't do any of that. They're better off over to John Doe's house where they can get his or her whatever they are on.

That's where they need to be, for what I can see because it wasn't happening on my watch. For as much as we give, much is received from the Lord. Mostly it is taken, but nothing is given because the church is a big marketing network today. All they do is business but not a godly business. They follow the lust of the flesh, and nothing else matters to them. They do it so smoothly in the name of the Lord, and that's the only time He is in it is when they use His name for the roots of their evil and call it the house of God, but it's not about God but only a show of their lust.

They are working in witchcraft and evil within them, what is supposed to be the house of God, but it's not of God. But if the churches were doing what they were supposed to be doing and the numbers that I see them pulling in everywhere of worshippers; well, let's say the world should be becoming a better place, and not a worse place because of all those are supposed to be servers of him. Instead, all that one truly sees is out of God, and it is wide open in the house of God today, and He is not pleased with this situation. People think they are fooling God, but they ain't and when a true man or woman of

God is invited to some churches, let's say: it's their first and last visit because if you're preaching and teaching the truth, they don't want you back because they want to keep the people right under their control. You might just give an eye-opener unto the people of God sitting before you, and somebody is going to question that you just brought forth in that ungodly place. God may have sent you there to shake up some stuff, and you didn't even know, but you just did. I was talking to a preacher today, and we discussed the same thing. He said how sometimes people who say they are of God, treat him poorly after receiving the message. Well, I find something wrong with that.

If I walk out the same way that I came in, they didn't teach me anything, and I wasn't convicted by anything in the message, well then it's not the place for me. You should always have some reactions from the pool pit. Something should have hit you, but I see people just as nasty as they were since the first time I said praise the lord to them. And ears have passed, and they still have no respect. Now, they are leaders of the church in all places.

Let's keep it real, they are living nothing, so how could you learn from them? What? Then you find people taking part in some services where one might ask, wasn't that excellent service, and they don't even know what it was about but can tell you what someone was wearing and stuff like that. Now, if that ain't crazy, I don't know what crazy is, but I do know who they are. God can't dwell in these uncleaned temples, and He doesn't lie, but people do all the time. They are supposed to be your brother and sister in Christ, but you can't trust them even when you're looking at them.

They are supposed to be your friend, but they don't even like you. But for me, I play the game knowing who they are, and who they aren't fooling as well. You better watch where you bring your titles into the storehouse as well because if you sow into the unstable ground, then you're not going anywhere fast, believe that as well. You must sow into the harvest of God, to truly be blessed. I've planted into the big time money preachers before. I'm no different from anyone else but God seems to lead me to the little hole in the wall church, and I find the people are down to earth just like me and we have the same type of love of God, within our hearts, and we all look forward to getting up and going to work in the morning. They don't know my testimony, and it's not always that important to share, but God lets His blessing go forward on an as per need basis. When God touches my heart to share, I do. Mostly, I just want to praise him along with them and have a Holy Ghost time in the Lord, for He and He alone is worthy. When you find those simple little people who just want to serve God, you better get with them. They are sincerely hard to find.

The others can tell me about the events, but they don't even walk, talk, or carry themselves as a child of God because you can't fool God, with the suit. It's all the work of the devil in all high places, and you better reach out and test your faith in God to lead you to another level in him. When that small still voice comes, and give you advice, you better be listing to him for God always sends the warning before the storm, if we are listening to him. Sometimes, no matter how hard you try to fit in you don't, and there's a reason that you don't, it's because you just don't belong there.

God knows, and he doesn't let you sit leisurely. When I was talking to this preacher, I was sharing some things that had happened to me, and I said them in private. The next thing I knew, they were all over the church, and I'm no fool and understand how it got there as well. I once told someone that they couldn't hold water if I put it in a glass, they would spill it because they can't keep anything. Then there are times that I had something to say, and I gave it to them, the mouth of the south because they would tell it to anyone who would listen, and that's funny too.

You genuinely feel as if you already know them and feel as if they should be in diapers because they are always changing on you. Before you can lay the phone down, it's already making its rounds and not in your favor. Now, remember, these are the big wheel church folks, so what could you expect from the little people like me? Just hope that you have good favor from the Lord because the odds are definitely against you in the church. When you have done all you can do, then you sit back and wait on the Lord to give you overflow for all that you have done for Him, and not them. Sit back and wait on the salvation of God, and that's more than enough for you. He will never leave you or forsake you in no form or fashion in Him. In these times, this is when kingdom principles kick in; for God releases the favor of Him within your life, and on my events, I truly feel the love of God from the people of God, who I invited into my home. It also lets me know where I stand in Christ as well because, on the average event, I can get more people and love and peace in my home than some people get in a church on Sunday morning.

Wow, isn't that something, and I'm not that important to me, but in God's eyesight, He gives me great favor with Him. He covers me in so many daily ways, and all I can say is: thank you Lord for coming to my aid and saving me, for You and You alone made me worthy. I will rebuke the devourer for your namesakes, he shall not destroy the fruits of your ground; neither shall your vine cast her fruit before the time in the field saint the Lord of hosts. When it's truly time to move, God will move you. You sometimes can't see it, but he sends people to pass by your way, and let you know what you're doing wrong.

God Sends Us Warnings before the Storm

I met a guy about six years ago, and this person had warned me about a man that I had met. He tried to tell me not to marry him, and everything else that he knew about him. Well, if I had been listening to him, then I wouldn't have ever had my husband number seven. He told me so many things about the walk that I was getting ready to take.

But as usual, in the natural eye, he and so many more of my family and friends had told me things, but I was so headstrong on trusting the things that this man had said to me in the name of the Lord. Well, so he said, God brought this guy in my life to give me a warning, they said that they still don't think I should marry this man from things that they saw and knew about him.

Well, I probably could have seen some of it, if I was looking for it, but of course, I wasn't, so I missed it. But today, I'm listening to the ones that I believe God had spoken life for me in my ear. They have been warning me again, and today I let the minister know I hear him, and I'm listening to him. He replied: it's about time. Now I don't think that this man wants me for himself. He's a nice looking guy and a hard worker as well; whenever he sees me, he's always speaking life for my soul for salvation purposes. This makes him stand next to me, to be a man above men to me. No strings attached, just the love of God at hand in his work. There are times that I would see him on his job, and all he's talking is the blessing and grace of God in his life, and how the church is over and it's genuinely kingdom time. The time is finished for playing church, but it is time to indeed seek God and all of His righteousness.

When you walk up on some people where you can feel the true anointing of God on them, well, you better be listening to them for sure. Then there are those others who just went because I don't feel anything on them nor receiving anything from them else too. But when I told him about my prayer to God to show me this man that I thought was the one, well, let's say I didn't like what I saw. Be careful what you pray for because sometimes you can't handle the truth. Food for thought, God will never steer you wrong in nothing, and again, He wants more for us than we want for ourselves. God got you if you're listening and walking by faith and not by sight.

Faith will carry you down roads that you've never ever seen before. It carries you within challenging times of your life, and you wake up and don't even know how you got there. But you know you did, and grace and mercy allow you to stand still and trust God. It's because of his grace you're now standing on, and not left alone on your own. When people try to speak things into their life, God is on the action, and you see it happen right before your eyes, and you know what you know because of He and He alone is the only one that can do that.

Life has put me down too as I have earlier described. Each time the grace and mercy of God have come to my aid, letting me move ahead. Healing starts when you start asking for grace, not when you resign to your fate. If you say you can, you will and if you say you can't, you won't, and the call is all yours to make. Praise is what I do. That's in my home and on my job and in the grocery store, it doesn't matter because I'm not ashamed of God because He's never ashamed of me. Some people act as if they only know you at church. That's telling you who they are for one, and for two, how they live. And let's not talk about their dress attire altogether.

The things that they wear are horrible, and when it comes to Sunday morning, they change gears. Some attempt to dress the part, so long if you don't see them on the other side of the door, and others just do what they do, regardless of where they are and don't care what anyone might say about how out of order they look, well, it doesn't matter to them.

They are truly within their comfort zone, and even the ministers allow it because of who they are as well, let's say they enjoy the chase and the catch as well, so don't look for them to say anything but keep the offering plate rolling. For the, it's all about putting in the offering plate, and if you're not contributing, let's say there's nothing left to talk about in their minds.

Well, I'm with Jesus 24/7. I dress the same and praise the same everywhere I go, and people who know me can assure you that I walk the same too. When I began to start getting my life right, the first thing I had to do was start with my thinking patterns. Remember, what you think is what you become eventually. Then when you get your mind right, slowly but surely, everything else falls into place. I do believe that when God gets through with me, he'll give me a husband that I deserve, one who is a true soulmate. A man who knows how to treat his woman the right way. Then, who knows how to respect his wife as well. Then whatever we have, the unity will become one, by not trying to sell me on what a man he is, but his actions will speak louder than his word.

Anybody can speak the words that one might want to hear, but living up to those words that flow out of one's mouth is something else. He will make me the delicious apple of his eye, but not one of the apples in his eye; because when I looked in one man's eyes who had asked me to marry him, in his eyes, I saw apple trees. A tree can provide you shade, but I found him to be shady.

A tree can't feed you, and he had never given me a meal or even acted as if he could provide one for me in the future. If you talk to a tree, it can't speak back to you, and this was the way that we were, with me never receiving anything of value from him. It was a waste of my time talking to him when all he did was spreading gossip about me. It includes many lies on me, making it impossible for me to build trust. And last but most of all, a tree can't hug you back and spend it's loving arms around you when you need it most because he felt he didn't have time no matter what you may have asked of him. I received zero effort coming from him, and then he thought that he was the Adam for this Eve, me? Well, of course not! That's why God allowed me to see all the branches in his life and know him for who he was and not who he said that he was. So I can't be the one for him, regardless of what he tried to sell me. I'm the one and only one for the man nominated by God for my needs with his grace and mercy. So make sure that God sends it to you, and it just didn't come to you for whatever reason, but you say it was God.

God never makes any mistake, but we do all the time, especially when we are out of God for sure. Then that's when you know who was called, and who just went. You then also know about people who are just trying to send you a message for their worldly gain and why? And I'll be wondering where they do that and who do they might do that with? Nevertheless, it definitely doesn't work with me. This is the best time to trust God and ask for his favor when you are having trying times in your life. When you have a lack of understanding within the things that are being put before you, you need to ask for God's mercy and grace. It doesn't matter who it is, your family or your co-worker or the members at the church, in all things you do, you need understanding in God. It helps you to grow and move forward in him even if you achieve no other benefits. Always remember, those closest to you are the enemy's best tool to use against you because you're not looking for it from them?

Always remember the love of God is still in our hearts at all times for his people, so the people in the so-called church today are the most significant users and will take the best from you first. It can be a homeless person or anyone else, and we naturally want to help them. I understand it's not always because we think we are better, but since we have a love of God for the people of God and want to help them according to His will for them.

If it's in your heart, the overflow will come naturally. God has more for you than you ever have room to receive from Him. The blessing and anointing keep falling down from high up on to the people of God, from the Father himself. You always must find your place in Him and hold firm and fast unto the words of God; in spite of everything else that might cross your path. He kept you first in the kingdom of God, and now you can see all his righteousness and blessing flow, for I have and I'm that testimony in His mighty works. The power of God has saved my life, then the grace and anointing followed as I walked in Him daily. So when the bills are high, and the cash is low, I just trust God.

People say I don't need anything but how foolish do that sound when they say that I have everything, and that's crazy as well. Yet, when they say I have everything, they might be half right, because I've got Jesus, and I don't need nobody else in my life to guide me. He has the most exalted name above all names, and He's the only one that can provide unto you everything that you might need or want, and He's enough for me.

The God I serve keeps with me in all the wrong decisions that one makes in one's life, even when we didn't take the warnings about the storms. That's how I felt genuinely when I got bit once again. Sadly but true, this was the worst nightmare that I ever had with the title of husband.

You name it, and he did it for sure, and God wasn't present in any of it at all. Well, he alone slowed me up from number eight. But definitely I saw the game before it rolled out on me, and I'm good for sure today and happy too. It doesn't take much sometimes for a wakeup call on what's good, and what's not so good in one's life. Indeed, that's one to grow on for sure. They are out there, and that salesman that's not out for any good, but it's up to us not to get sucked in by them.

12) And all nations shall call you blessed: for ye shall be delighted within the land, said the lord of hosts.

-Malachi 3:12

Guidance for the People of God

God blesses us in our coming in and going out in Him. The praises go out within our lives for Him, and He always sends small signs of wonders within one's life. People that you may pass in your path know that you are blessed without you saying a word. They know who you are, and what you do in the name of God. And that little light called the glow of Jesus, well it shines everywhere you go. People know when you walk into the door, who you are, and those devils flee from you as well. When you are protected, God sprinkles the works of witchcraft away from all around you. You're always on their tongues, so you know that people think about you and you will find that they talk about you as a result. Just keep on doing the right things and move forward because God is not through with you yet. Your blessings are in the air, so reach out and stand firm on God.

The word of God is for the people of God to guide them in the right path as they walk. They can get mislead as well, this is so true because we all fall short of the glory of God, but again God wants more for us than we want for ourselves, only if we are listening to him. So many people don't know the voice of God because they're caught up in man and his foolishness.

It's so true, they miss out on His path laid out for them. I know people that spent so much time practicing to learn how to serve God or His word. You name it, and they've been doing it, but the true spirit of God isn't there at all. And that's sad because they might miss heaven by way of the so-called church that they are attending for grace and mercy. The big money market churches are all over the place, but what's with the salvation of God? They aren't teaching anything, and they aren't living something of substance too. Both sides get what they put in it, and then they think that the church is over for them. Their walk isn't right, their talk isn't either, and there is no presence of God. But that's the reason they don't know because they don't know God, and when they see you blessed with something, anything they try to talk about you or the look on their faces is worth a million words.

This occurs since they can't hide what they feel inside, and it shows on the outside all too well. When you see the actions of some churchgoers all the time, and then you never see the fruit of their labor, while they are still buying food stamps and stupid stuff like that. You might wonder who are they truly serving, and why they find nothing wrong with any of their actions at all.

Well, just take a look at them and how they are living, and you can't help but wonder, do they think stealing from the government is of God's will? I don't! I think someone's children will be hungry before the end of the month, and these people played their part in making these children go hungry with their stealing. They use handicap tags because they are too lazy to walk, but someone handicapped is put to a disadvantage because of them as well. They already have things going on in their lives, at least when I was handicapped, I knew what it felt like on both sides of the street; the before and the after. There are some things you might not want to speak into one's life, and that's one of them, so I don't really know which God they serve, and neither do I want to learn either. They have no respect, not even for themselves lest anyone else.

There are things that I used to do wrong which is so true, but after going through so much, I've learned to do better in every walk of my life. I can't ever think about going back unless it's to keep me pushing forward in Christ. He is the keeper of my soul salvation, and I walk in him at all times. Some people say I'm nasty; this is their opinion of me, but generally, I'm not. I can be pushy which is true, but you got to bring it to me first. You shouldn't put out what you don't want back, ever. The word says: do unto others as you would have them do unto you.

So don't get mad because you didn't expect me to react that way, but you were asking for it. So I gave it back to you, and this isn't godly either, but it is the flesh of man doing its work as it always does in people. Jesus would have turned the other cheek, but I didn't. Sometime after the storm, we must go pray for our actions that occurred out of God and know better, but people will push you there. This happens if you allow them to affect you.

And I stand to be corrected, God always wants better for us than we want for ourselves in all parts of our life. Today, I was talking to one of my ex-husbands, and it's not like today was special because we talk almost daily, for it is his daily bread at most times. Well, he was speaking to me on forgiveness in my heart, something that if I'm honest about, I really don't do correctly in God.

He made me take a look at myself from his eyes, and I had to agree with him because I knew the things that he was saying was so true. He made a point about the lack of trust that I have in people and forgiveness as well when they do things that I don't like. Well, there was nothing he said was wrong about me but sometimes you've got to check the mirror for yourself as well. He knows the word of God backward and forward, and he touched on how he got caught up in the flesh in our marriage. If he didn't, he knows he would still be here happily married to me. I'm not so sure about that because what God puts together, no man can tear apart, and when it says man, it's speaking of mankind, regardless of gender. As the word of God doesn't lie but people do!

So, what I received from the talk was that there is still hope for me in God for renewing of the status of my life called marriage. No, I won't remarry anyone who I have been with, in the past, but trust God to send me who He wants for my life. I've been told that before by many men that God sent them, but it wasn't Him because actions speak louder than words. I believe that the word of God is the only truth and everyone else is a liar.

13) Your words have been stout against me, saith the Lord. Yet he say, What have we spoken so much against thee?

14) Ye have said, Its vain to serve God; and what profit is it that we kept his ordinance, and that we have walked mournfully before the Lord of hosts?

15) And now we call the proud happy; yea, they that work wickedness are set up' yea, they that tempt God are even delivered.

-*Malachi 3:13-15*

I've found times in my little life, where people have spoken evil and wickedness against me without a cause. This is so sad because they don't even know my real name but drag me through the mud anyway. They do this to people all the time without any reason at all. They don't like the color of one's skin or the way their eyes are slanted, and the list goes on.

Perhaps if they had taken the time to learn about that person, they would have felt differently. But they don't they just go on hearsay? What a better world this would be if people understand this statement alone. Stop judging people but learn the spirit and heart of the man, again I'm speaking of mankind, male and female.

I've seen times someone told me that I was mad at the world and so evil, and I just didn't feel that way when I met you today. Well, they were not judging you according to someone else, but the person standing in front of them, which is godly! This is the fundamental way we should do everything in our lives, but we don't. The wickedness is sitting in high places all around us, and you miss it if you're not looking for it, and that's how you fall in the trap that the devil has set up for you as well.

He will sell it to you, and it sounds so good, and you get caught up if you're listening to it, but what did God say for your life? Well, let's say you better be running behind God and not man. When we look at people, and they say things that we really can't get where they were coming from, it might not be you but them alone. They have issues that you don't know nor can see, and they couldn't be talking about you, but themselves in the situation.

I find this to happen quite often in people. They take their own shortcoming and then spread it around like grass seeds all over the place. They don't mind who they hurt in the process because they are hurting so bad themselves. They only want someone to feel what they are feeling as well, so they cut anyone who comes in their path as if they are not good.

They are standing beside you on the altar call, but they aren't giving it to Jesus. They find fault in everyone else except themselves, and they don't understand why they don't have any growth within their lives at any point. The beginning is always seeing yourself before you can see anyone else. Taking the blame for one's self before pointing at others and when you realize who you are and make a claim to your own shortcoming, then you're done a great job.

Then they that feared the Lord spare often one to another: and the Lord hearkened, and heard it, and a book of remembrance was written before him for them that feared the Lord, and that thought upon his name.

-Malachi 3:16

Some people don't even fear God in anything in their lives, and the reason you know this is by observing how they do things in His name. They have no shame in their games, not at all and no repentance either within their lives. They live, talk, and walk any kind of way in the Lord. They are all around us today, and the ones you least expect are the ones that bring the cruelest trick of the enemy, believe that! They are so good at it, they could sell you back the same story you just told them with interest.

They sound so good and sweet that you buy from them without one question asked because first, they sold you their idea. The rest came easily after that. Oh, but God is just not like a man with weaknesses, so He knows and doesn't fall for the trick of the enemy at all. If you're where His mercy is, then you wouldn't fall for any theatrics either. He allows us to see the trick of the enemy if we're looking for it. The spirit of God knows all our weakness as well, and that's when we should be praying more before we make any wrong moves in our lives.

I know there are times when we move before thinking things out properly. I am at fault for doing that all the time. I look for the good in people, but the truth is that there isn't any good in them. Not for any reason at all! But one thing's for sure, God knows that I tried to put faith and trust in them. I found a phone that was missing for weeks.

I know where I left it, and I know that I went back to get it, and it wasn't there as well. Well last Sunday, I showed up at my office to give someone the stuff that I was holding for them. After we parted ways, my phone showed up in my purse. Now I've been in my purse daily since the phone was missing.

But today, it showed up. What's one to think about this? Did the person have it and returned it? Did their conscience bother them? Did they realize that they were cutting the hand that was helping them? Only God knows because I surely don't, but one thing I do, it wasn't in my purse before today.

And they shall be mine saith the Lord of hosts, in that day when I make up my jewels; and I will spare them, as a man spareth his own son that serveth him.

Then shall Ye return, and discern between the righteous and the wicked, between him the serveth God, and him that serve him not.

-Malachi 3:17-18

Believe me, God knows the difference even when you don't, and He and He alone makes corrections in our lives for our good. He has promised us to always catch us whenever we start to move away from Him. God wants us to remain close to Him and follow His word in life.

He wants us to strive for them the best, even when we fail to consider it as the most viable option. He holds his promises open for us, but most of us are looking for nothing but a quick fix for everything. We forget the part about the long suffering. Well, let's just say we won't want to work on that. But when we give our lives to God, we think it should be easy street from then on, but that's not true, not at all.

Things might get harder before everything becomes more manageable in one's life. I've been there and did that as well. I've lived through the rough roads we call life! It's not so gravy now as well, so some days are good, and others are not so good.

But at least, I have my eyes open to the enemy and recognize his tricks for what they are, and keep it moving forward in favor of God for my life. It is only possible with the dose of mercy that Jesus delivers to me repeatedly. Sometimes you don't question anything, but just stay focused as you move forward, because the outcome is the glory of God. He is just waiting on you to do His work, but He doesn't depend on you to keep Him waiting.

The favor of God shows up in so many ways, and in most cases, these are ways that you're not looking for. It could be in a small child; it's no telling who God may use for presenting His mercy in one's life. Sometimes, I've heard children say things today that make me take a second look at them, and pay attention to them quickly. They do nothing as I might have done as a child. They don't play the same, and they don't desire to do it as well.

Of course, the time has changed, along with everything else, but how we played together and shared, most of the kids today have none of that. It makes them selfish and the parents today make them that way as well. They never teach children to share with one another, not even with their brother and sisters. Unity isn't in the household, and I didn't really explain my kids much either, now when I think about it. Well, let's say: I had given them toys, but what they really needed was love from their mom, and I missed out on it!

Money couldn't buy what they needed the most, and so many kids have two parents, yet the homes aren't any better for them. The parents are never at home raising the kids. They rely on the after-school programs, coaches, and teachers to do the job for them, and the kids don't get what they indeed are in need for.

They need the love and care from their parents, which is greater than anything else that they could possibly have. I look at my grandchildren, and during and after school and even summer breaks, it seems as if they got something to do every day. I know their parents take them to the movies and dinner, but mostly they cry out for one on one time. This is much needed today in the fast life. I realize that I missed it as well, and my kids are somewhat different from their parents because of the lost time. They do work, but those sons of mines are fathers above fathers when it comes to their children. We do learn what we live, and today, I'm still doing that thing called work! Today my children are all grown with children, and I see the family curse, in some ways, are still going on. I don't have anyone to work for, but me. But if I could have done things differently, I know that I would have.

But it's too late for that and today I just watch the outcome of my grandchildren from afar. I find myself sometimes pushing away because so much has already been put in their minds, about me, and for me, I watch as well as pray for them. Prayer always works in our favor at all times in Christ. He is the keeper and brings the restoration in our family, our job and anything else in our lives. I'm a witness to that one as well. I have found that His mercy falls in so many small ways that benefit us.

Chapter 3
Learning Who Not to Trust

I allowed someone to put my car tag on, and they didn't apply it right. Now, I've allowed them to do other things for me, and I've always had the same results from them. Now if I'm paying you, I do expect to get my money's worth, but in this case, after they finish, you're looking for someone else to come cleaning up behind them. Well, when I say God gives small favors, he gave them today.

When I arrived home from work and went to open my car trunk to get some stuff out that I had just brought at Walmart, my license plates fell on the garage floor. All I can say is that's you, Lord, helping me out. It could have fallen anywhere from my home to work and back, and I travel more than thirty miles each day. But favor let them fall in the garage for me. The tag wasn't lost, and it took only a few dollars to replace the screws, which is a blessing. It could have been lost, and a police report had to be filed, and all that stress of the ordeal. So daily, I give praise regardless of the task put before me, or things that just come within the daily task for me. God always gets the praise and glory. God has everything to do with it, everything! God's blessings are missed in some cases forever. Some people would have called that luck, but me, I say God's mercy was at play. Usually, people would have looked at it differently. They would have said something like this: man, I was so lucky today, I almost lost my tags.

Sounds like the average person, right? But as a child of God, we give credit for everything that God does in our lives no matter how big or small; only He gets the praise out of it. I find myself above average because I feel like I can't praise him enough, and the more I do, the more I want to. I thank him for every dollar that I make; I don't take grace for granted at any time in my life. When I run across the takers and not the givers, I do know how far to let them go with me as well.

Like the guy I was talking about and my tags. Now he did some work for me, but I learned really early that he was a talker, rather than a worker. He changed prices on the same job three or four times before he had finish talking. My Godly thought had kicked in at the start, and

God had told me not to trust him, but again he was selling his self so hard, I truly missed it that first thought of God for me was not to trust him. And I trusted him to start doing some work for me at my home. I chose the wrong answer, and now I'm waiting to see him in court. Well, let's say this that he finished half of the job, so he owes me money. The job has never been thoroughly done, so now he's on the run from me. He doesn't answer the phone and fails to realize that I can get to him any day of the week that I want, I do know how, but it's not that serious for me, so I let him slide, now that's God's mercy for him. He made such a bad name with my neighbors as well that they don't want him in our neighborhood.

Some people thought he was working in here for me first, but that wasn't true, just first on my street. Anyway, when you make a name for yourself whether good or bad, it sticks and sticks hard. Somethings you can fix and others, you never will, and he's made such a bad name in this subdivision, I don't think he will ever be able to fix it from where I see him at now. The jobs that he did, people just like me had to pay someone to redo them, and he puts all the blame on the people, never looking at himself. I take pride in my job because my customers know that I'll be there after they complete a sale. Sometimes they come back and whatever went wrong happened a year ago, and I'll still fix it for them just to make them happy. Although they ripped their pants or broke the strap on their bag overloading it, nevertheless I'll fix the problem for them without any fuss. They get happy, and I'm glad that I could take care of what I was doing for them. This is a good business practice, and this guy couldn't do good if you put it in his hand and spelled it out for him; he would still mess it up.

That's sad because he'll give you all the exercises in the word but never correctly do anything right. But if you're listening to him, he has the greatest sell pitch in himself that you'll probably ever hear. It's all good coming out of his mouth, but his actions are something else. Please don't let him start telling you on how his mama raised him; that's another book altogether. He says how he was taught to do things right and speaks highly about his mother's upbringing of him, but his actions tell another story.

My kids' friends always tell me how great they are, and what they see in my kids as well, and what they see of me in them as well. Most of the people that work my older son are old enough to be his father or grandfather, and they always tell me of the kindness in his heart for people. Well, I know that because at that moment, he's truly being his father's child. That's the actions of his dad for sure. He services people in business with pride, and that's genuinely his mother as I take pride in everything I do for people.

It's always good, clean business or no business at all, and I do look for it in people, but most people just don't have that in them. They say they know God; they say they are always thanking God for the blessing of him, but their actions speak differently. I believe that because if they were acting in God, then they wouldn't be in hiding after the job they have done. I know I couldn't sleep at night knowing some of the stuff, I've seen people do, I couldn't imagine living like that! No peace, no time and having an excuse about everything that they do, and always putting the fault on the other guys, but this isn't saying much about you either.

Food for thought: if you have a business, you must always be in your business to make it work according to your standards, and the people that you sometimes put your faith in will fail you, which includes family, friends, or some John Blow on the street corner. They all drop the ball sometimes, but you should always own up to mistakes and fix them instead of dodging them as this person does.

The world is full of them in all kind of high places, and you know them by names, so I don't have to call them out. You already know who they are and how they work as well. It only lasts for a while, and then they all come falling down eventually. This is called everyday life, and the faces change, but the game doesn't, and some never learn from their mistakes.

This was a high priced one for me, but for me, there's no hate on anything in my heart because it was one of those cases where God told me not to fool with them, but of course, I did what I usually do. I didn't listen to God, and it cost me a lot, and the price of the lesson was truly well worth it. I've been set in my way for so long, but God is grooming me in His way, and I'm starting to get it. When He says don't go, well I'm listening and not going. And when He says stop, I'm stopping. Most of all when He says: that's not for you, believe me, I hear Him, and I am learning to listen hard to the voice of God because the outcome is too costly otherwise. God keeps us on track when we obey his voice unto us, but when we keep doing what we're doing that's when free will kicks into our life and creates a mess.

God don't make messes, but people do and blame it on him? If I could roll back the pages of time in my life, including all the marriages and different things that have taken place that I had control over, I would do them differently for sure. But the mercy of God has kept me standing firm in Him for all of my shortcomings. Grace wakes me up each day with more prayers of faith for today's journey in Him.

Looking for What Can't be Found!

Therefore leaving the principles of the doctrine of Christ, let us go on unto perfection; not laying again the foundation of repentance from dead works, and of faith towards God,

Of the doctrine of baptisms, and of laying hands, and of resurrection of the dead, and eternal judgment.

And this will we do, if God permit.

For it is impossible for those who were once enlightened, and have tasted of the heavenly gift, and were made partakers of the Holy Ghost,

And have tasted the good word of God, and the powers of the world to come,

If they shall fall away, to renew them again unto repentance; seeing they crucify to themselves the Son of God afresh, and put him to an open shame.

-Hebrews 6: 1-6

The message of these relevant verses remains that it is important to look for repentance and find guidance. I've found that in today's churches, a lot of the pastors or leaders or whoever they are supposed to be, don't make altar calls. There is no laying of hands on the people, and I've questioned this because there have been times I wasn't feeling well myself and was looking for it when I arrived there. I found no movement of God within those walls, not even in the people present within the walls as well; they were all dead unto the spirit of Christ. All I wanted was to remove myself quickly because you must watch the places you attend and the spirit that lays before you as well. Sometimes, it's not suitable for your salvation. In such cases, just flee, and flee fast before the spirit of them hits you hard. See, I've been on both sides of the street.

I was raised up in the church but later learned that the church had to be in me. It requires the practice of living, honoring, and serving God. It's a life walk. Going to church means nothing, nothing at all, but living honorably unto Christ does. Once you make the shift change, there's nothing you can do wrong and then feel okay about it.

I say nothing because God doesn't allow you to rest when you know you've done wrong, but you have to go back and get that thing right! That's in everything! When the commitment is right, you naturally do it. But when you're so used to doing wrong, you're always okay with anything that you say and do to people. That's in the church and on the street corner because you're being who you are, and people see you for who you are as well. I guess that's why when they are in the church for any service or rehearsals, I can't understand why they don't turn off their phones. They think that they can't miss a call. I've seen them on the pool pit texting and doing other foolishness there. But God, if they only knew him, they should have given Him that quality time instead of giving to those who can't do anything for them, without Him.

That's one to grow on truly, as Christ is everything. It's unfortunate when people try to call themselves, walking in unity when in a relationship. They think that they got it all together, then the big rain storm comes in one's life that they aren't prepared for. Well, this was a customer today. Last year, they came in to get their uniforms for their job. They were telling me how great life was. They had just finished law school and got their bachelor degree. Not only that, they were going back for their masters. Then they went on to tell me how they got a new home and a car as well. I was so happy to hear the great news that they shared with me, for them.

I like to listen to the good news in people's lives. I get tired of, who got shot, who's in the hospital with some kind of illness, or who's now dead. When people are doing so nicely, well I always count that as the blessings of God and give Him the praise in their lives even if they don't. Well, today it's a different kind of story, and it began like this: CeCe, you're not going to believe this! First of all my baby sister found out she had cancer, and they gave her six months to live, but she died after only two months. Then my wife and I broke up, and I lost my new home and ended up on the streets homeless.

Well, that was only the beginning of his problems because his wife's son brought about the situation causing him to end up homeless. Then I shared with him that I understand about being homeless, because, I too had been homeless before. A lot of times, people are going through something, and they are talking to you as if you couldn't have ever been there, but you have. I then told him that one time I was homeless and had to sleep in my job. I went to the YMCA to take a bath there after my swimming classes every morning and night. He said her son was breaking into his neighbor's house and robbing them at gunpoint. So they put all of them out of the neighborhood. Then all his bills got behind including his truck note, and they're looking for it now. The only good thing was that his job gave him a raise and made him a supervisor. Well, I say that was the renewing of his blessing. Well, after that he just found a place to call home for now but didn't own anything anymore' no clothes or furniture or anything else. Well, this is the glass half full time again. The bright side is that he's still standing in spite of everything that happened and has a job.

He got a raise and a chance to move forward. The ex-wife is calling him now to come back, but I think if they do it to you one time, they'll do it again because of the lack of respect. If we were together since this child was young, and he wasn't trained to respect you, well he never will, and you're the only father that he knows. Really? Where do they do that at? With you, if you let them! These kids don't respect nobody, nobody at all, regardless of who they are or as they say: who do you think you are! Well, a lot of time you got to listen to

A LITTLE DOSE OF MERCY OF JESUS

someone, and this leaves my customer. Now I turn to talk about my grandson.

Love for My Grandson

You can't talk to him because he's the sharpest knife in the drawer, and his mother ain't no help either! She allows her children to have their way in everything. Then she finds no wrong and justifies whatever they do. Okay, he's headed for a lot of trouble with that behavior. Someone called me about him and the choices that he has made for himself.

Well, you can sell people close to you anything when they aren't looking for it, and that's his mom. Millions of parents do the same thing, they put their trust in their kids until they get locked up or shot. Then, *"Oh, my God"* kicks in, but when you could have listened to someone else, you didn't. It could have saved you from the day that you are now facing before you. Well, he's gotten in some trouble before, and he's not out of it yet, but that means nothing to him. Others care although he doesn't care about himself.

His girlfriend was calling me about some issues with him. I carried out the chain reaction; I called his father, and he called his mother, and his mother called me. Now, of course, I already know how this is going to go. Everybody is wrong, and he's right. But today, I'm not buying it! So, she's not talking to me about it. Same old broken record playing on just a different day of the week. Anyway, I told his girlfriend to help him as it will take tough love, so stop upsetting herself with him for one. Well, I'm not going back for anymore of the foolishness, never! I've outgrown the stupid stuff for real, and I'm not buying the stupidity, not at all.

Then she's all messed up behind him, but when I called his father, he stated that it's tough love time, and that's all he got left for him. I really didn't agree, but left it alone. Sometimes you find yourself caught up in things that you just don't want any part of. Well, this is one of those times. My grandson's girlfriend's mother called me because she was so upset with him, and you do want to give people the best advice that you can. Well, people smoke weed and do all kind of stuff and find nothing wrong with it, but it does have an effect on you. I've seen my nephews; the way that they act after they are high on weed or something else as well. Their whole attitude changes and everything else about them changes as well. Well, this is a part of my grandson's problems along with some other stuff. Well they say, it does nothing to you, but they can't stop doing it. I find it to be crazy because I'm not letting anything nor anyone take control within my life. I used to smoke cigarettes, and I put them down so easy. The first thing I did was stop buying them, and I've never been one to bum a cigarette from anyone, so I quit after that.

It's all in your thinking, believe that, and most people don't think this way. After they are all messed up, they might start trying to think about how they got there. Now, it's a little too late for that by that time. Nevertheless, you are all messed up in trouble and left wondering how you got there. My grandmother, on my mom's side told me at the age of ten years old that trouble was easy to get in; it could take no more than five minutes to get caught up and then fifteen to twenty years to get out of it. Well, she told this to me mainly because I used to be a fighter.

She called it silly fighting. You would be talking to me, and I would start hitting you, while you were talking. She said I was headed for trouble. I try to talk to my grandchildren as well, but they can't hear me because today they don't hear anyone.

They think that they are smarter than you and got all the sense in the world. They indeed are in so many ways because they have so much more than my generation did, but they don't use their minds for the greater good. They think they have all the answers, and they do; just that they are all the wrong answers to the life's daily tasks, and they try so hard to sell it to you as well, but you know better.

You are trying hard to make them do that stupid thing that people don't do today, which is to think! You can't help someone who doesn't want help for themselves. His girlfriend and her mother wanted more for him than he wanted for himself, and I told her that she can't keep fighting a losing battle. Although it is my grandson, I don't uphold anyone in their wrongdoing, regardless of whoever they are.

You never make agreements with the devil, and she was trying to do that with the words: I love him, and then I had to say: if you love him, let him go; you're taking yourself through so much, and she had been talking to me for more than an hour over things that he was doing wrong. Well, she wanted more for him than he wanted for himself, and he should know right from wrong. His mother is a minister, and he's been in church all of his life. That's when you let go and give him to God because He has more power in people's lives than you do!

I was looking back over my grandson's life. Well, he has been an usher in church and has enjoyed several facilities from the church including schooling and various programs for gifted students. The list goes on, and now I wonder how he got to this point in his life and on the path that fails to bring success, but jail and hell if he's not careful. Again, God wants more for us than we want for ourselves, which I keep repeating. Then people around you want more for you than you want for yourself as well. It's a never-ending problem for the ones that love you more than you love yourself.

They sit around and worry about you, and you go on happily doing what you're doing without a care in the world. You continue your worldly affairs until it all starts falling down. When you are going down by yourself, you then try to take everyone else down that road of nowhere with you. Now you're down and alone, but when they were trying to help you, you didn't hear them. Wow! When someone was trying to warn you before the storm, you weren't listening to anybody. But after the storm, you want to be welcomed with open arms? Now, that's how most people do, by keeping in and out of the church. They go to jail, and you go to prison with them as well. You both now got sentenced.

In most cases, so does their entire family. Well, that's not my testimony. I like to say you've been taught better, and I'm not running down there for your pity party when I warn you before you got to this point within your life. Most of the time, we find that time fixes everything, the good, the bad, and the ugly will come back to your remembrance. Some sooner and some later, but it's all happening. Believe that, and you of all people know when you see it again. My grandson got arrested for being on the wrong side of the expressway and sleeping in the car, probably high on weed. Now he has no license, and his girlfriend drives him around. So, I do understand her concerns about his smoking habit. On that first note, I helped him because my son asked me for help. Now my boys haven't been in trouble for anything like this, nor even other such vices. Again, God helped me to raise them with good role models around them as well. But anyway, against my will, but for the will of my son and grandson, I helped. Now, I'll never help with anything like this before. I am hoping he learned from his mistakes and not doing stupid stuff while on probation, or all that help goes for nothing.

Now his mother finds nothing wrong because she never does with her children and seems to cover everything with her favorite word (well). It starts out well; but well doesn't take care of anything, but she drags the word like it's the cure for everything. It's the word that she uses to cover up the wrongdoings of her children or anything else which is harmful. And all the churchgoing and everything else looks like it has been a big waste, to me.

Now she goes to a big church as well, and I guess it's like many churches, where people practices their ministry license as well, but how they genuinely live and their children is beyond belief. And now she has a grandchild, I can't help but to wonder, will he be raised with the same spirit of well, and will it still be okay for them? Now that's something else. We can't lead anyone when our home just isn't right. At least, that's how I feel personally. To get mine right, I moved by myself, and I'm not letting those ungodly spirits up in here.

Chapter 4
You Know the Spirit, by the Spirit

I found my small space in the world, and I'm not going back for anymore of the foolishness. Now some people never learn from anything, but keep doing the same thing looking for a better outcome. Well, it's not happening, believe that! You got to make that shift change within your life for things to turn around for you.

Keep doing the same thing, and you'll keep getting the same results. Personally, that's insanity to me. However, ninety percent of the world is living in what I may call madness. They get caught up in people's names of clothes, and they wear the spirit of skull heads like it's cute. Then the music that they feed their spirits is also something else as well.

They feed themselves the spirit of the devil, so well, and they can't see what's wrong with it and where it's taking them as well. You should have a standard for everything in your life. Everything has some kind of meaning for sure. People walk in spirits of the unknown for real. Sometimes they come past me, and I can feel the spirit so real on them, and I move quickly because I don't want that devil on me. Like some people don't think witchcraft is real, but it is. There are all kinds of spirits in the world, and they are all over in high places as well. Some spirits remain hidden, but you can find where most of them are if you know what you're looking at.

The spirit of God is the same way. Especially if you know him for yourself, then you know when you're in a good company or not. It's that simple; he lets you know and how far one has come and as well with those who are around you. The best part about God is the wisdom to see the difference in Him. The wickedness in the world is not as revealing unto the natural eye because the devil has to have them fooled to fall for him, and he gets them on.

A quiet note is that they have all the riches of the land, which is so true. They practice control and power over the place. This is a fact, and you don't mind because the gleam looks so good, you just got to have it. This seems to me because I know people that truly live and walk that way. What's wrong with me? No, what's wrong with you? That's the question that I'm asking myself, but I already know; no God, no peace, no growth in him, and you're running all the time down the road to nowhere fast. Sometimes I ask myself, why can't you see yourself? I surely can see you. You're never more than a dollar away from being broke, and never truly enjoy what you could have in Christ, for real. All I can see is that you're wearing out your shoes, and if you look down, you'll see you need some new shoes. Never able to keep anything one hundred percent in your life, you have nothing but always got some game to everything in your life, every time you open up your eyes.

You are never honest with yourself of all people, but you have sold yourself so many lies, you believe them? That's a real fool. And you call yourself blessed from God, but truly have no blessing from God, because you're not in a relationship with God, but only with yourself. People just use his name as a tool, to con people into your mess and get involved with you, wow! It's genuinely a common thing today that you see every day.

People walk around living in the shadow of themselves, and no one else knows who's for real or who's just out to get what they can, from who they can as well. I spend my time trusting no man but putting my faith in God for all things within my life. The Bible tells you not to trust a man. Man will fail you. Ask me, I know this first hand for myself, and people also share their stories with me all the time.

This will keep me making books of awareness for others to know that you're not alone. There are others out there but not talking to you, although they are going through the same challenges as well. And when I use the word well, it's not to justify what's wrong, but to create awareness about the problem of what's wrong with people.

You might have known some people for more than twenty years of their lives, but you may not know anything about their troubles and spirit. Well, looking out the natural eye, you may have seen other things that may not have set well in your spirit. That situation is in everyone's life, no matter who you might think that you are. They find fault within you but never in themselves.

This is so true. So when you start thinking you'll find stuff which is troubling you, you can still miss out. Your problem may be standing right in front of you, but you just let it pass you by. This happens all the time, but God showed it to us earlier before the storm, but we kept moving, and now we have reached a critical point. Now, all hell has broken loose, and you're lost.

Well, I'm found, as I've found a better way to deal with all the challenges of my life. Those people, places, and things aren't good for me. I've had to let all the *"its"* within my life go, and let God deal with what I know I can't. That's a smart way of handling those people who just want to have their way, and so I let them figure it out for themselves after I've given a warning sign to them, but they didn't listen.

First, I told my son on this matter that your son is a grown man, but you should provide him the necessary guidance to ensure he can stay away from vices. My grandson needs guidance in his life, and then I did what I do best, turn it over to God. I know my son loves his son, but I have to respect him too as I want it for myself. You can't get what you're not giving. Most people don't think that way because they are takers and not givers, and you're only their on an as-per-need basis for them. They are never there for you, and they also never offer you good advice. But I've been there and walked that line too.

So I'm now taking a seat and watching this one ride out. I do think that I might know a better way, but I'll let the smarter ones handle their messes and see what the end will be. I may discuss this in my next book. God's grace has everything to do with it, and the mercy of God will always get the glory in the end.

His favor in your life weighs out the odds for yourself in Him because you of all people know where you stand. It is something you can't fake because God knows when others don't. You can't fool God at any time, but you can make a fool out of yourself all the time.

Moving Forward

For if the firstfruit be holy, the lump is also holy, and if the root be holy, so are the branches.

And if some of the branches be broken off, and thou being wild olive tree, wert graffied in among them, and

with them partakest of the root and the fatness of the
olive tree.

-Romans 11: 16-17

Everything turns out good for the work of the Lord in our lives. It's all within the matter of time; have due time and due season, and the good within one always turns out for the good of them. You can't love and pray for all people, and God doesn't bring them out to an awakening in Him.

He said to raise a child the way he is to go, and when he gets older, he won't depart from it. Well, this is sure a case like that. My grandson has been taught better, but he's not doing better. Now, what will it take to open up his eyes, well, only God knows because I truly don't. I'm just praying it's sooner than later.

I don't want him caught up in some criminal activity, but he's heading that way. People who know him want better for him. I know my family isn't unique. We have had the drunks, the drug addiction, and all the other things that you find in a typical family. But yet we have had more preachers and leaders for guidance to know better as well. Nevertheless, we have also had some twisted up preacher kids too. They sleep around and do the things that they were taught better to avoid. Some of these things that I learned about them, I learned from people in the streets out of all places. I learned more from their co-workers about the ungodly things that go on with them, but nevertheless, I didn't know the things they told me but had no problem believing them because they might be closer to them than me.

Also, you know co-workers, and people on the street see them more often than me as well. Some of my customers tell me things that are going on in my family that I don't know. Like a week ago, a customer came to buy a security uniform for her husband and told me that my nephew had a beautiful baby girl some weeks ago. Well, he didn't call me to tell me that, but if he needed some money he would have made the call for that, wow! I learned about his first child's birth from a customer. Now his mother didn't tell me, and she's my sister. His brother called me days before she came in, and he didn't tell me either.

But a customer whose husband is his friend told me, then something is truly wrong with this family for real. Again, I just sit back and watch the fake people within this family just roll on by me. They are so artificial that it's a shame, and I know that my parents taught all of us better, but the choices we make for ourselves re something else.

I'm glad they aren't here to see what this family is coming to, in the next generations. I don't even understand how they got so far off track myself, while I was sitting here as well. However, they always have a ready excuse for themselves by blaming someone else for their shortcomings.

They keeping finding problems that they can associate as occurring because of others but never seeing who they indeed are and the fault lies squarely on them. If I see it, why can't you? Because you're not looking for it, that's why. God knows you for your works, and they aren't good either.

Game Changer

Game-changing situations can occur at any time. Here, I want to describe what happened with me on July17th. I just left one church and was sitting in another one, waiting for service to get started. Well, I felt that the first service was truly moved by the spirit of God. The pastor's wife brought forth a true message for the people of God on today's service. She didn't have to open up a bible because the word was in her already, and she brought forth a good lesson. If I didn't know better, I felt as if she was reaching out to me and me alone, but the word went forth for all who could receive and benefit from it.

Well, it was a holy church, and God was moving within those walls. He had a way with the ones who could receive him. The others were lost as usual. Well, her husband the Bishop had been on some missions for God. He had just got back last night from preaching in another state and had to preach at another church this morning as well, but he still made it. He wasn't missed by me because the lady brought the spirit of God in the church with song and praise and spoke His powerful word for all. Anyone looking for anything other than that missed what God had for them today. That's easy to do when you're caught up in other stuff and are not at the church for the right reasons. That was part of her message, and I genuinely received that from her as well. She might have made the devil mad when she said they play Russian roulette with their lives. I do believe that as well in so many small ways. People truly don't know how to serve God, but he's always there for them.

When her husband arrived, he said she had already delivered a mouthful, and there was nothing that he could add further behind her, and I truly agree with the man of God in this regard. She left no rocks unturned, especially if you were paying attention to her. She found times when she had to remind the people of God what kind of church it was.

We enjoyed its holiness, and we clapped our hands to make a joyful noise unto the Lord, but many were not acting like they were in a holiness church. This I do know so well because when I'm in other churches, I clap and dance and then the people there; they act like something is wrong with me. Well, it is, and you need to get a hold of some of it for yourself. You don't understand then why you're never blessed. I know because your praise isn't right. They need to go back and check themselves and get it right before God. At least, that's what God wants for all of us as well. He keeps on moving in your favor regardless of whatever we do ourselves. Everything that might happen in one's life, the good, the bad, and the ugly occurs as well on their behalf. Well, my second service was musical. It was quite lovely, and the spirit of God was also high in this place.

So, if I may say: it's a glorious day in the Lord. The Bishop who the musical is for seems to be quite pleased from where I'm sitting, and I only wish the best for him within all things unto God because that's who it truly is all about. I find that so many people miss that part in everything that it's all about Christ and His message. He gets the praise and glory, for He alone is worthy, but we seem to make things all about us, and He's looking for praise and glory. You learn this as they talk, and they got it so twisted when it comes to me. I'm a true runner from all the stupid stuff.

But anyway, that has nothing to do with this musical. The point is still quite important because we get caught up in the music and miss the meaning of the song. They listen to the beats and miss the message within it. This happens all the time regardless of where you are. The places change, but the game always remains the same for them. Maybe we should always be doing things unto God and not unto man.

That's always going to be your shortcoming in God when you miss out on His message. You can never beat God's giving, no matter how hard you may try. We can run but cannot ever hide from God. We can try to miss him, but when God wants you, he knows where you are. God will always have the final call, in all things, believe that as well.

I've been here too many times before, and the spirit is trying to move in this place. Some people are always going to be who they are, and you cannot change them, but even when you know who they are, you can't let the devil steal your joy in spite of them. I really didn't feel it, but I pressed on because as a child of the Lord and when the devil tells me don't go, I really know I'm going because I don't let him get any victory from me if I can help it. So I'm here and enjoying the service that is being put forth on today. It's too hot in here for me, but I won't let the devil get the victory in that way either. Today, is not your day with me Satan, not at all today, come back tomorrow, and press your luck then. God's not dead but very much alive within me if nothing else, and he says I'm worthy, so I just keep moving in him.

When this day is over, I'm going to get a good tonight sleep, I'm so tired, and I'm feeling it as well, and all I can say is God has been good to me today. Moreover, I can't wait to get up and go to work in the morning because that's my daily prayer. It's funny because people pray for lottery numbers and other things, but never for work.

When you enjoy the fruits of your labor, you'll understand what I'm talking about. It's a blessing just to want to get up and go to work when I can remember that I couldn't when I tried to in the past. Now, that's true food for much thought in Christ, the healer, and the restorer of your life. When you look back from where you come and see where you're standing now, that's a blessing itself of the power of God. If you have had the shoe on the other foot, you would understand. Nobody can take your joy, and I know it because they can't take mine as well. They don't even stand in my way, period. They just don't understand, yet until they get there, and then and only then will they know. Some get it quicker than others, and some never get it because it's not everyone but only God who wants everyone to learn and live according to His word and will in their lives.

18) Boast not against the branches, But if thou boast, thou bearers not the root, but the root thee.

19) Thou wilt say then, The branches were broken off, that I might be graffed in.

20) Well, because of unbelief they were broken off, and Thou standest by faith. Be not high minded, but fear.

21) For if God spared not yet natural branches, take heed he also spare not thee.

-Romans 11: 18-21

Love Has Everything to Do with It!

Sometimes you can put more on you than you can bear. That's not a good thing, and when you allow others to overload you, that's even worse. When we allow ourselves to be put into situations that we already know are bad for us from the start, we cannot get good returns from our labor.

Today after the musical, the traffic was so bad I decided to stop by my uncle John and aunt Catherine's house. Now I call them from time to time but honestly don't visit them much. Anyway, my uncle John who is a minister, always give us time together whenever I drop by to see my aunt, Catherine. Then from the time whosoever opens the door, we chat, and today it was uncle John, and he said something about the shoes that I had on. We followed it up with our usual girl talk. Well, I sat to talk with my aunt Catherine, but as I got ready to leave, my uncle John wanted to borrow my shoes. He wished for my aunt to put on some heels, being that she doesn't wear heels and take a picture of her legs from the knees down. Now I thought that was just beautiful.

Mainly because after fifty-eight years of marriage, let's say he still got love and feelings for her. It was really a pleasure by allowing her to put on my shoes, but I was more than happy to see her in them as well. When we looked at the pictures, her legs looked as good as mine, and she is old enough to be my mother. I now smile when I think about it. She and my uncle, I'm sure haven't had the perfect marriage because there's no such thing as that, but I've never heard a cross word between them in my life.

Today, it was like any other day to me. They respect each other, and when she doesn't truly agree with something, she doesn't say anything but gives this little look that lets you know she really isn't agreeing, but ain't saying anything. What kind of love they have always had for each other surprises me and cheers me up. Now she is that delicious apple within his eyes, and when she looks back in those eyes, all she sees is the same thing. After all these years, they still have love for each other that God wants for all of us to have with our soulmate. This is an excellent example of a soulmate if I've ever seen one, and it's quite close to me as well because it's in my family. My mother's parents were the same way, and only death did do them part as well, and my grandmother, was indeed the little girl next door. Now, that brought me to another level as well. When and only when God sends me a husband, and a true soul mate, let's say I want him to be like my uncle, John Smith, or my grandfather, Emory Bryant. These are true men of God, who genuinely loved their wives and had true respect in their hearts for their soulmates. He doesn't have to have light brown eyes like my uncle John, not at all, but have the true love of God in his heart, for the woman of God in his life. And the respect should come naturally at all times within his life.

You can't hardly believe it but they still got it, after all these fifty-eight years, and it still shows within them as well. She was like a Christmas tree, with all white lights lit up as he took the pictures of her legs and feet in those shoes and said she can't wait to show them to her youngest daughter. Well, I said: don't show her, she will be too jealous. That was a joke because they are indeed close to all of their children. They are as people say: thicker than thieves.

But it's truly the love of God within their hearts for each other. I think that there is nothing greater than to have love among family members. And in this family, most of the people are so fake and don't respect each other at all. Ask me, as I used to be one of them. That's some more books to come where I will describe how I was.

I woke up one morning and said: today is the day that fakeness ends, and it ends today with me. So if I don't want to do it, well I truly don't. If I don't want to go, well I am not going, and the list goes on. It was all out of God anyway, so let's keep it real and one hundred percent, all the times. That's the Godly way, by keeping it for real unto him because he knows your heart.

Anyway, life becomes a whole lot better when you are true to yourself first and then with others, if nothing else they must respect your mind for who you are. Some people had the act of godless but are truly so far from it. They will get you with the manner of Godliness, as they talk to you and carry on with you, but you got to know the difference, and if you're watching closely, you'll quickly see them for who they are as well. I know I did, and I have love for them as God requires of us; nevertheless, leaving them right where they are. God wants us to love and be kind to all of his people, because He did, and we are no better than Christ himself. Like the man and his wife, I told him to speak and be kind to her no matter what, when she calls and even though he said he's done, she kept calling and trying to go out with him, and that's okay. I do it all the time, but meanwhile, I know I'll never be involved with them in a relationship, no more than that.

You have to draw a line on the foolishness. If you don't, they will come back to tear you down some more, but you don't ever let them get that close ever again. However, you should continue to show the love, in spite of whatever they have done to you because God honored that action of love, from you to them as well. Not what they think that they were going to do to you next, because it just failed.

Now some people never grow up, at any point in their lives. I was talking to a friend who finds me unbearable when it comes to sleeping around. She is hard on the actions of the sin within her life and feels that the Bible has it wrong. She thinks that you shouldn't marry anybody that you haven't slept with, but my understanding of the word is, if you save yourself for marriage, then you have nothing to pair it with. You've never been looking for anything because you don't have anything to compare it to or feel that you're missing something. You're a virgin, and he's a virgin, and you guys will love and learn each other, but I never wondered about all the stuff that I heard coming out of her mouth. I do know people who met each other and lived happily married for more than fifty years, and they are friends of mine.

When you hear their love story, it's very touching. She feels that there is nothing wrong with casual sex. And no doubt because when you truly don't have God in your life but still a churchgoer, then it's a comfort zone for you that you will defend aggressively. It's that simple, the devil got you all caught up, and the preacher should be preaching it, but if he's in it as well, I do understand it. Some things aren't even spoken on in the church because the leaders are right where you are as well. They don't preach on the games that they are laying themselves. She wanted me to stop saying that I'm not going to have sex before marriage, and it's crazy to marry someone who you haven't been with. I think it's crazy to lay with all those men and not once have a husband, and you don't know why. Well I do! You are good enough for the night, but he doesn't want to wake up with you each morning. I tell women all the time when they wear their clothes tight, and they tell me that they are looking for a husband.

Well, he's going to sleep with you, but he's not going to take you home to meet his mother. And a real man looks for a woman of the same class as his mother, but if she too was a street woman, then you got it made. Now that has never been my problem, but I see it all the time, and I'm not going to stop saying, it's better to marry than to burn because marriage is honorable in God eyesight; but if you genuinely don't know God, I do understand. It's all over the world, and many men and women don't find anything wrong with this, and they are all sitting in churches of all places, never getting corrections in their lives as they walk out the same way they came in.

Now, that's the American way of serving God, and he's never in it at all but flows off of their tongues, as if he was okay with their sin ties.

Pulling Yourself Forward

7) In the night did God appear unto Sol'-o-mon, and said unto him, Ask what I shall give thee.

8) And Sol'-o-mon said unto God, Thou hast shewed great mercy unto Da'-vid my father, and hast made me reign in his stead.

9) Now, O Lord God, let thy promise unto Da'-vid my father be established: for thou hast made me king over a people like the dust of the earth in multitude.

10) Give me know wisdom and knowledge, that I may go out and come in before this people: that is so great?

-2 Chronicles 1: 7-10

Little do we realize, greatness is in all of God's people if we are listening to ourselves! In most cases, we are too scared to try, or should I say, we lose our faith in us. Second, we want it but don't want to work for it, that's the most significant shortcoming on our behalf. And it is too bad because God already put that in your DNA, and you put that other thing in like: lazy, sorry, don't want to work for the things that you wish to get or just don't honestly try. So many people are their worst enemy. Nobody else has to do anything because people set out to hurt their own selves, so you don't have to.

They make sure they always keep themselves down and still a dollar away from being broke. Then you got those real runners in Christ. They are firm believers and will always work to follow the word of God until the last drop of sweat falls from their skin. They run like I've heard some people say a Jamaican run. Why the Jamaicans? Because they are hard workers.

They will work two or more jobs to get what they want. Now, that's not all of them of course, but I do know some people personally who are really hard workers and good business people as well. Of course, I know some that do hook and crook in business as well too, but the good ones outnumber the bad ones, all the time. It's what you want and can make out of it always.

God made promises to David, but also unto you as well. We must always walk by faith and not by sight. Always trust the words of God and never a man to see the promises of God. Be strong-minded first of all and apply the will of God unto every walk that you take in Him. Don't ever let the devil steal your joy. He can always get in your way, but he can never stop you unless you and you alone allow him.

This is the promise of God. He never said we wouldn't go through, but we will be overcomers in him. The grace on David fell down on his entire family and his children's children. We have the same opportunity today, and that's to make it either right for us or no better good at all. We should open the welcome gates to the power and the glory of God, but again that's not what people usually do in their lives albeit going for the opposite.

I'm on a lone battlefield, and I'm always fighting hard to keep my head up high. I want, just like Jesus, more for people than they might want for themselves. I give open-heartedly, but I get rejections on everything under the sun. Sometimes I try to be a blessing to the church and the people of God. This is so true within everything that I attempt to do. It's funny how they act when you're gone. They are lost for words, and it shows all over their faces. You do know what a difference a day will make, not in some things, but in everything.

But, oh when you truly understand the God you serve, you're always doing good in spite of the whispers on the walls. If walls could talk, well you probably wouldn't like what you might hear. But, I always say in spite of everything, God has your back. The Lord gives us wisdom and knowledge to always know the difference, as we make the shift changes within our life.

Like when you can sometimes see people with things, but you personally do not have to have it, but others drink Hater-aid because they don't have it, but want it. I say why don't want to apply themselves toward what it takes to get it. For example, it might be the car that you are driving or the suit that you are wearing. Then you know who they are, and then you can stay away from them as well. I've never seen someone with anything they had, that I felt I personally wanted it.

I like to say that I do like it for you, but personally, I don't have to have it, now that's me. Anything that I want, I'll apply my time to work for or give up something to get something else; now, that's me as well. For one, it says how much I am willing to make a sacrifice for it, and when I receive it, I know that the commitment was within me for it and the favor of God for me is to have it as well.

I can remember the times that I've given up food to buy something else that I wanted. As I said, I wanted it, but maybe I didn't truly need it. Now that's crazy, but the flesh will make you do stupid things, and for me, that was one of them at that time within my life. Today, I see myself much differently. I told a friend of my ex-husband about the apple in my eye on yesterday.

His reply was so unexpected. He told me how he took it, and when he finished, he had seen it on another entirely different level than me. He said that he used to think about tracing women, meaning that he undressed them with his eyes, and how men trace woman is that they don't just look at them but have body movements as well. They start from head to toe and look at their butts and everything. They completely undress them with their eyes. Well, he said that he doesn't do that anymore. It had cost him a marriage. He said that he had outgrown that action six years ago. Now he's forty-four years old. So he got it quicker than most men. Some men never abandon the stupid stuff and fail to realize why they never have good relationships either. They see a woman and have to talk to her and try to sell their innocence to them. They are happy as long as they can get away with whatever wrong they may be doing. When they get caught in something, then it's a different story.

Well, I know this only too well, as one might say, first hand. I expected more from the men that I married, but nevertheless, they were who they were. Then regardless of who they had married, that was it. They would tell a new lie daily, one behind another to cover up the truth of who they were. They will make a fool out of you with their lies if you let them. I've been wiser in this case because again, that daddy that I had taught me what to look for in some instances, and believe me, I did back then, and I still do today as well. I'm not going to act as if, some of the things that I went through, didn't have any effect on me because they did. In most cases, my life with one of those husbands who couldn't tell the truth if you put it in their hands, they would still tell a lie and say: I didn't see it but holding it. Now that's bad but so true. Perhaps, it was just as one might say: that was his way of doing things, in spite of what effect it had on the other person involved with him. It didn't matter for the people around him or the ones that knew him well.

His own mother had tried to warn me about him saying: I know you are going to want to kill my son but don't, just send him back to me because all those women that he had wasn't always wrong, but a whole lot of it was honestly him as well, and the stuff that he took them through was terrible as well.

I learned who I had married after I had said I do. Since we got divorced, he has had another child and other interests. If I had thought it was bad enough when I was married to him, let's say the big show is still going on full force with the actions within his life. Also, sad but so true, he is so proud of the man that he is. Well, that's him, and everyone who knows him will tell you that you can't outtalk him nor out-hoe him either as well. It's true, what's in a man will always come to light. Of course, in his case, the lights are always on high beam and show everything. Now don't think he doesn't attend church as he comes from a family of preachers as well, but some of the sin ties were in that family as well, and nobody found anything wrong with it! To let him tell the story, it was all good in the neighborhood. I don't know if it was because his grandfather built it or because his grandmother accepted it. Anyway, I had to tell his grandmother that I wasn't her and will not put up with all this foolishness in him.

Now, he was named after his grandfather. This was so true, but I wasn't any way like that grandmother with him in any way. I found her to be sweet and gentle and kind to me, and everyone who knew her; but I would never wear her shoes. Not for one day! And that got me to end up on the side of the road, and today, I can still see the scars on my body that remind me of how far God has brought me. Moreover, when I think of the goodness of God, I say that's more than enough for me.

When his friend reminded me of his last visit to me, of course, I didn't remember and said how he tried to tell him of his action in our marriage, but he won't listen because he always had to be the big show. It reminded me of when he asked me to marry him, and my mother wanted to know what I saw in him. I told her that he talked more than me, and when he spoke, I just sat and would be quiet.

She didn't find that to be a reason to marry someone, but I allowed him to sell himself to me, regardless of what the others had said to me about him. I must say: I should have listened to them on that note because they were right, and I was wrong for trusting him. Well, I hope that his new wife gets better treatment than I did, and if nothing else, respect that a wife deserves.

I've heard the story, but won't speak on that but you know something's just ain't worth talking about, and he's one of them. I've let go and let God have the final say in all the ex-husbands I have had in my life. I am still looking to see the glory of God for me in that area of my life because there are the hope and promise of God for everyone who wants it, and I do want it. I don't look like what I've been through because God restored me with his favor on my life. And when his friend saw me, he said, how good I looked since he last saw me, and I had to give all the credit and glory to God. For without God, I would have been long gone, but God showers His mercy of me. When you know how far that he has brought you, how could you not want to serve him?

1) In the Lord put I my trust: how say he to my soul, Flee as a bird to your mountain? 2) For, lo, the wicked bend their bow, they make ready their arrow upon the string, that they may privily shoot at the upright in heart. 3) If the foundations be destroyed, what can the righteous do?

4) The Lord is in his holy temple, the Lords throne is in heaven: his eyes behold, his eyelids try, the children of men. 5) The Lord trieth the righteous: but the wicked and him that love the violence his soul hateth.

6) Upon the wicked he shall rain snares, fire and brimstone, and an honorable tempest: this shall be the portion their cup. 7) For the righteous Lord Lovett righteousness; his countenance doth behold the upright.

-Psalm 11: 1-7

Our eyes hold so much in them. Mainly the truth. When someone is trying to lie to you, you can read their eyes if they give you eye contact. I had asked a man one day to remove his sunglasses. For one, well, we were inside, and I wanted to see his eyes. He didn't remove them. He said that stars keep their glasses on all the time.

I really didn't understand that because for one, he wasn't a star, and that didn't make it right; but anyway I just left it alone. If he felt like it was too much to ask, so be it, and I kept it moving. Some battles are not worth fighting at all, so I pick and choose my battles wisely. The eyes open up the sins in people as well. Because they don't look like who they indeed are. They may walk as a profit of God.

They may talk as if they know Him quite well. But how they are living is what counts in the end. Some devils are so good that they can look you in the eye and lie perfectly.

They will sell you rain on a sunny day. They are that good but what does God has to say is the only thing that truly counts. The righteousness in a man will always show up for who he is, and the sin as well will come forward, and you'll know exactly who they are as well. God always does everything with favor for your good. Then the blessing always comes with favor for one's life.

Sometimes, it doesn't seem as if it's for your own good, but at the end, the good is correctly shown up in Christ, for all of the favor of Him and the mercy that He offers to us. Bless be the name of the Lord, for God is good, all the time, and all the time, He's worthy as well. I speak peace in the land among God's people everywhere because these are indeed trying times, and it's trying times everywhere you might look to find peace.

I heard a girl in the store on Saturday say that she was going to Africa. Now, she's from Africa as well. She said she took the whole month to visit her family because it was too much for a week. Well with the things, the way that they are going today, she'll be lucky to get back in the country. I've heard of other stuff like that. Some people got in but couldn't get out. Again, it's trying times all over the land, and if we ever needed a prayer, we need it now.

God is sitting on His throne awaiting on us to come to Him, and not Him coming to us because He already knew the state of the land. He knows everything before it came unto this day and was trying to get His people ready, but they didn't take heart to His call on our lives. Some are praying, and others are still living the same way as they always have. It is sad but very true in times like today.

"Preserve me, O God: for in thee do I put my trust"

-Psalms 16: 1

All of one's trust must be in the Lord, at all times in one's life. He is the keeper of our soul and salvation belongs to Him alone. He is the one that giveth, and he is the one that takes it away. Bless be the name of the Lord, for He is worthy.

1) Hear the right, O Lord, attend unto my cry, give ear unto my prayer, that goeth not out of feigned lips. 2) Let my sentence come forth from thy presence; let thine eyes behold the things that are equal. 3) Thou hast proved mine heart; thou hast visited me in the night' thou hast tried me, and shalt find nothing; I am purposed that my mouth shall not transgress. 4) Concerning the works of men, by the word of thy lips I have kept me from the paths of the destroyer. 5) Hold up my goings in thy path, that my footsteps slip not. 6) I have called upon thee, for thou wilt hear me, O God: incline thine ear unto me, and hear my speech. 7) Shew thy marvellous loving-kindness, O thou that savest by thy right hand them which put their trust in thee from those that rise up against them. 8) Keep me as apple of the eye, hide me under the shadow of thy wings, 9) From the wicked that oppress me, from the deadly enemies, who compass me about. 10) They are inclosed in their own fat: with their mouth they speak proudly.

-Psalms 17: 1-10

When we are the apple in Gods eye, we are glorified in him. Not that things will not come and go within one's life, that's not true; but if we humble ourselves unto the Lord and remove our spirit of pride, then we may humble ourselves unto Him. The soft spoken voice of God is sometimes missed in our life.

God is always talking to us, but we're not listening to Him for the favor of whatever is on, on our plate. At least I know I have missed God too many times to talk about it, but I am still learning to take the voice of God to heart.

The footsteps of Christ aren't easy to follow, but you become worthy to walk in his path that provides you mercy. They are an everlasting journey, with endless tasks of always trying to stay ahead of the enemy's tricks. The wicked will always fall in their own nets, always.

"But the meek shall inherit the earth' and shall delight themselves in the abundance of peace"

-Psalms 37: 11

This scripture says a lot. The meek in God shall inherit the earth, so it doesn't matter how else people live. If they believe they are better than you, they're not! It's all in their minds but not in the eyesight of God. He has a masterful plan within His hands, and He knows about their shortcomings.

1) God be merciful unto us, and bless us; and cause his face to shine upon us; Se'-lah. 2) That thy way be known upon earth, thy saving health among all nations.

3) Let the people thee, O God, let all the people praise thee. 4) O let nations be glad and sing for joy: for thou shalt judge the people righteously, and govern the nations upon earth. Se'-Iah.

5) Let the people praise thee, O God; let all the people praise thee. 6) Then shall the earth yield her increase; and God, even our own God, shall bless us. 7) God shall bless us' and all the ends of the earth shall fear him.

-Psalms 67: 1-67

God is always merciful in all things He brings to us. The blessings continue to fall from my mouth in all conditions. We should always make a joyful noise unto the Lord, praising him for all things that come from Him. Everything that breathes should praise the Lord for He is kind and worthy.

Search me, O God, and know my heart: try me, and know my thoughts: 24) And see if there be any wicked way in me, and lead me in the way everlasting.

-Psalms 139: 23-24

Deliver me, O Lord, from the evil man: preserve me from the violent man;

-Psalms 140: 1

1) Lord, I cry unto thee: make haste unto me' give ear unto my voice, when I cry unto thee. 9) Keep me from the snares which they have laid for me, and gins of the workers of iniquity. 10) Let the wicked fall into their own nets, whilst that I withal escape.

-Psalms 141: 1, 9-10

When you realize who the *"its"* are within your lives, things will become great in your favor. These evils can be the people that you might hang around or just talk to on the phone; that's not any good for you. The *"it"* can be a close family member, who never have your best interest at heart in all aspects of your life. It can be the child that you once held in your arms, and today, they lay heavy on your heart.

And last but most importantly, they can be the one that you took for a soulmate, yet you now realize that you have nothing in common. How funny but true that people can make significant changes in your life with minimal effort. Sometimes you get the chance to walk away, and other times, you die with the hurt still on your heart.

But God can help release it all in His mighty name. You can escape and become a champion in Him. The wicked can't prosper in the evil that they might have set out for no good for your life, but they always set up a trap for themselves instead.

Conclusion

As I bring the Volume I of Mercy to a close, my hopes lie in the fact that you spirit keeps on guiding you. You just have to know your spirit. The end of Volume I is not the end of the way of life I intend to show my readers. Read Volume II to discover how God changes your life and yet some people twist His words too!

CECE

www.ingramcontent.com/pod-product-compliance
Lightning Source LLC
Chambersburg PA
CBHW021127020426
42331CB00005B/651